111066

BCFTCS

DISCARDED FRO

D0994029

From good intentions to good practice

Mapping services working with families where there is domestic violence

Catherine Humphreys, Marianne Hester, Gill Hague, Audrey Mullender, Hilary Abrahams and Pam Lowe

In association with Barnardo's, The Children's Society, NCH Action for Children, NSPCC, Women's Aid Federation of England and the Child and Women Abuse Study Unit (University of North London)

The POLICY PRESS

First published in Great Britain in August 2000 by

The Policy Press
34 Tyndall's Park Road
Bristol BS8 1PY
UK

Tel no +44 (0)117 954 6800
Fax no +44 (0)117 973 7308
E-mail tpp@bristol.ac.uk
www.policypress.org.uk

© The Policy Press and the Joseph Rowntree Foundation 2000

Published for the Joseph Rowntree Foundation by The Policy Press

ISBN 1 86134 245 4

Catherine Humphreys is Senior Lecturer, **Audrey Mullender** is Professor of Social Work and **Pam Lowe** was research worker, all at the Centre for the Study of Safety and Well-being, University of Warwick. **Gill Hague** is Research Fellow and **Hilary Abrahams** was research worker, in the Domestic Violence Research Group, University of Bristol. **Marianne Hester** is Professor of Sociology and Social Policy, at the International Centre for the Study of Violence and Abuse, University of Sunderland.

All rights reserved: no part of this publication may be reproduced, stored in a retrieval system, or transmitted in any form or by any means, electronic, mechanical, photocopying, recording or otherwise without the prior written permission of the Publishers.

The **Joseph Rowntree Foundation** has supported this project as part of its programme of research and innovative development projects, which it hopes will be of value to policy makers, practitioners and service users. The facts presented and views expressed in this report are, however, those of the authors and not necessarily those of the Foundation.

The statements and opinions contained within this publication are solely those of the authors and contributors and not of The University of Bristol or The Policy Press. The University of Bristol and The Policy Press disclaim responsibility for any injury to persons or property resulting from any material published in this publication.

The Policy Press works to counter discrimination on grounds of gender, race, disability, age and sexuality.

Cover design by Qube Design Associates, Bristol
Front cover: Photographs kindly supplied by Karen Bowler, The Policy Press.
Printed in Great Britain by Hobbs the Printers Ltd, Southampton

111066
B.C.F.T.C.S.

Contents

Acknowledgements

From good intentions to good practice has proved to be an ambitious project to undertake in a nine-month period. The fact that it has been achievable is due to a high degree of cooperation at a number of different levels:

- between the six women on the research team;
- with the participating organisations who coordinated the research in their agencies – The Women's Aid Federation of England (WAFE), Scottish, Welsh and Northern Ireland Women's Aids and the children's charities: Barnardo's, The Children's Society, NCH Action for Children and the National Society for the Prevention of Cruelty to Children (NSPCC);
- with representatives of the statutory agencies in England and Wales, Northern Ireland, and Scotland;
- with specialist researchers from the Child and Woman Abuse Studies Unit (CWASU), University of North London and WAFE who conducted aspects of the research on our behalf, and the London Research Centre;
- with the large number of workers from projects and organisations who took the time to fill in and return 915 lengthy questionnaires;
- with workers and service users from the projects which generously agreed to participate in the case studies;
- with the Joseph Rowntree Foundation who funded the research.

This complex and enriching collaboration has been a remarkable process and the research team is greatly indebted to all the participants, especially the four children's charities, WAFE and CWASU who all undertook specific pieces of work.

We would especially like to thank the members of the Advisory Group: Christiana Baafuo-Awuah (London Borough of Newham), Helen Bullock (Department of the Environment, Transport and the Regions), Sheila Burton (CWASU), Nicola Harwin (WAFE), Enid Hendry (NSPCC), Annie Mullins (NCH Action for Children), Anne Van Meeuwen (Barnardo's), Ann Wardell (Cleveland Multi-agency Forum), Celia Winter (The Children's Society); Sarah Mulholland, representing Aaron Poyser (Department of Health); and Susan Taylor, Senior Research Manager for the Joseph Rowntree Foundation.

Some of the people to whom we would like to express our particular appreciation include: Ennis Nicholl in Northern Ireland, Claire Houghton and Alison Stephenson in Scotland; Judy Williams, the researcher with WAFE; Charlene Craig and Violet Greaves from Northern Ireland and Welsh Women's Aids respectively; and Margaret Shapland from the University of Bristol Computing Service.

Introduction

This project was carried out between January and October 1999 with the aim of establishing the range and extent of service provision across the UK for families where there is domestic violence. Specifically the project set out:

- to identify and map examples of family support work with women, children and men within both the statutory[1] and voluntary sectors throughout the UK;
- to identify innovative work in relation to domestic violence and family support in both the voluntary and statutory sectors;
- to develop a framework through which examples of good practice can be identified.

A team of nationally recognised researchers was assembled to conduct the study. Gill Hague and Marianne Hester (the latter now at the International Centre for the Study of Violence and Abuse at the University of Sunderland), of the Domestic Violence Research Group at the University of Bristol, and Audrey Mullender and Catherine Humphreys from the University of Warwick, have previously undertaken national and international research studies of domestic violence as well as consultancy, teaching and training (Mullender and Morley, 1994; Hague et al, 1996a, 1996b; Hester and Radford, 1996; Mullender, 1996, 1999; Hester et al, 1997, 1998/2000; Hague and Malos, 1998; Hester and Pearson, 1998; Mullender and Humphreys, 1998; Harwin et al, 1999; Humphreys, 2000). The Women's Aid Federation of England (WAFE),

Sheila Burton from the Child and Woman Abuse Studies Unit (CWASU) at the University of North London, and the major children's charities – National Society for the Prevention of Cruelty to Children (NSPCC), Barnardo's, NCH Action for Children and The Children's Society – have all participated in the study as collaborators. Active links with the Social Services Inspectorate (SSI), the Scottish Office and the Northern Ireland Health and Social Services Trusts have been drawn on, or developed, in respect of work undertaken in the statutory sector. Overall, this project represents a unique, innovative, collaborative research effort.

The project has aimed to reflect current national thinking (see for example, Women's Unit of the Cabinet Office and Home Office, 1999; WAFE, 1999a) which views domestic violence as a crime and believes that support to survivors is a priority. These ideas have been translated into two overarching principles which have guided the work throughout. These are:

1. The development of policy and practice which directs responsibility to perpetrators in relation to their abuse.
2. A commitment to work with domestic violence survivors – (usually) women and children – from diverse backgrounds to ensure their safety and well-being.

A related aspect of the work has been the emphasis placed in the qualitative (case study) phase of the project on speaking with survivors

---

[1] For the purposes of this report, statutory sector refers to services provided through local authority social services departments in England and Wales, social work departments in Scotland, and health and social services trusts in Northern Ireland.

directly rather than only listening to the views of professionals.

Background

The aims for the research grew out of the particular context of domestic violence work in the UK. Since the 1970s, when the first refuges opened for women and children escaping violent men, there has been increasing public, policy and professional concern about the issue of domestic violence. The scale of the problem, and its consequences for women and children in particular, have been gradually recognised. Research has also highlighted the major financial implications of domestic violence for local authorities and services (Stanko et al, 1998).

The 1990s have seen the development of services within the statutory and voluntary sectors geared to work with and support families, and individual family members, where there is domestic violence. Research in Northern Ireland (McWilliams and McKiernan, 1993) and Scotland (Henderson, 1997) has pointed to the rapid proliferation of services for women and children in situations of domestic violence, while also highlighting gaps and inconsistencies between and within departments and organisations.

Work with and support for families

An accurate reflection of the range and extent of work with families where there is domestic violence requires a broad view of practice and provision. The notion of family support is usually seen in the context of provision by social services for children 'in need' under Section 17 of the 1989 Children Act or Section 22 of the 1995 Children (Scotland) Act. However, in relation to policy and practice, the development of services for 'children in need' has tended to be uneven, reflecting the lack of a commonly applied definition (Tunstill, 1997) and the fragmentation of service provision in the UK. The notion of what constitutes a 'family' in circumstances of domestic violence is similarly unclear. It may mean: (abused) mothers and their children, (abusive) fathers, mothers and their children, or more extended family networks (Gittins, 1985; Hester et al, 1998/2000). It is therefore important to include the variety of definitions of 'work with', 'support' and 'family' which are used by agencies dealing in all aspects

of domestic violence: in essence this encompasses all work which does, or could, relate to children's family life and women and men's parenting roles.

In the UK, the development of work with and support for families where there is domestic violence has developed in a number of directions. The period since the 1970s has seen:

* work with (primarily) women survivors of domestic violence;
* work with children living in circumstances of domestic violence;
* work with both mothers and children;
* work with (usually male) perpetrators of domestic violence.

Work with women survivors of domestic violence, mainly in refuges but also elsewhere, probably has the longest history with regard to family support. Over the past 20 years, the main specialist providers of services in the UK for women and children living with domestic violence have been Women's Aid and other women's refuges and outreach services. They have managed to provide innovative work for children and have built up a body of knowledge and expertise (Debbonaire, 1994; Hague et al, 1996a; Scottish Women's Aid, 1999). In the last 10 years, this work has been built on and supplemented by policy and service development throughout the statutory and voluntary sectors.

Increasingly, and largely as a result of the work outlined above, the provision of support to mothers (usually as non-abusive carers) now tends to be regarded as the most effective child protection strategy in circumstances of domestic violence (London Borough of Hackney, 1993; Mullender and Morley, 1994; NCH Action for Children, 1997). Recent policy initiatives and practice directives have reflected this. Following two conferences on the issue in 1995, for example, the SSI report on *Domestic violence and social care* pointed out, "Protection and empowerment of non-abusing women is effective child protection" (Ball, 1995). The Department of Health (DoH) Circular on Part IV of the Family Law Act similarly suggests that "[w]here domestic violence may be an important element in the family, the safety of (usually) the mother is also in the child's welfare" (DoH, 1997, p 12). However, recognition of the woman's needs does not imply that these should be conflated with children's needs. They are linked, but separate, and intervention needs to flow accordingly.

The emphasis on work with women as mothers builds on an increasing recognition of the complicated connections that often exist between domestic violence and child abuse. Research from the UK and elsewhere has shown that abuse meted out to mothers can adversely affect children in many ways, including their self-esteem, their relationships and their behaviour (Parkinson and Humphreys, 1998; Hester et al, 1998/2000). Children may also be at risk of physical and sexual abuse from the domestic violence perpetrator. They may be caught up in the violence and be abused in violent incidents against their mothers, or the same abusive pattern which men may use towards their partners may also be used towards children (Casey, 1989; Hester and Pearson, 1998). Increasingly, domestic violence is being seen as an important indicator that a child is 'in need' and may be likely to suffer significant harm (Hester et al, 1998/2000).

During the 1990s, the need to support children living in circumstances of domestic violence was identified, for example, by the DoH. A number of the studies in the DoH's *Messages from research* on child protection (1995) indicated that domestic violence may be in the background for up to half of children experiencing abuse. Support for children living in circumstances of domestic violence was also emphasised through the DoH commissioning of *Making an impact: Children and domestic violence* (Barnardo's et al, 1998; Hester et al, 1998/2000). With regard to policy, the DoH Consultation Draft on *Working together to safeguard children* (1999a) states that it will often be appropriate to regard children in situations of domestic violence as 'children in need' (para 6.37).

The 1995 Social Services Inspectorate report also highlighted the desirability of providing services to this group of children through early intervention and support rather than investigative enquiries (Ball, 1995). The children's charities have made similar pleas based on their own experience, and have since been active in developing family support services where there is domestic violence (Abrahams, 1994; Mullender, 1996; Hester and Pearson, 1998). Children's rights to support and assistance in all abusive situations are, of course, highlighted in the United Nations Convention on the Rights of the Child (United Nations, 1989).

In the UK, the growth of work with men who are violent to their female partners is relatively recent.

This began to develop partly as a result of policies aiming to recognise domestic violence as a crime, and in response to a growing recognition that more interventions need to be aimed at men as the cause of most domestic violence (Mullender, 1996; Hague and Malos, 1998). Programmes are run chiefly by probation and the voluntary sector, and limited success in stopping men's violent behaviour has been claimed (Dobash et al, 1996; Burton et al, 1998). However, such programmes are only just starting to address the impact of men's behaviour on children, even though most of the men concerned are probably fathers (Hester et al, 1998/2000) and there are relevant models overseas (Mullender, 1996).

It is also important to recognise the role of multi-agency initiatives and forums with regard to the development of work with and support to families where there is domestic violence. Hague and Malos (1998) and Hague et al (1996b) have charted the development of inter-agency responses to domestic violence in Britain, while policy level support has come from the National Inter-agency Working Party Report on domestic violence (1992), the Scottish Home and Health Department (1990); the House of Commons Home Affairs Committee Inquiry into Domestic Violence (1993), the Home Office and Welsh Office (1995) circular on inter-agency work and domestic violence, the DoH (1997) circular on the responsibilities of local authorities in relation to the 1996 Family Law Act, the Home Office (2000a) Circular 19/2000, and the new Home Office multi-agency guidance (2000). Domestic violence forums are particularly important to an overview of family support work as they may coordinate and collate information on relevant services.

The DoH's revised draft of *Working together to safeguard children* (1999a) indicates the importance of creating clearly defined links between multi-agency domestic violence forums and Area Child Protection Committees (ACPCs) (para 6.40). In the ACPCs' reports from 1992 onwards there is evidence of an increasing awareness of domestic violence as an issue of concern for children, although with less evidence of effective intervention (Atkinson, 1996). The Local Government Association has prepared a briefing for its member authorities on domestic violence and child protection (Mullender and Humphreys, 1998), again highlighting the links between issues for women and issues for children. Other initiatives by government will also create an impact on family support services in this area. These include: the audits of local crime and disorder problems (including domestic violence) under the 1998 Crime and Disorder Act; initiatives arising from the report on *Policing domestic violence: Effective organisational structures* (Home Office, 1999); the inter-departmental review which is over-hauling funding arrangements for all forms of supported housing, including refuges for women and children fleeing domestic violence (DSS, 1998) ; and the initiatives arising from the Crime Reduction Strategy (Taylor-Browne, 2000).

In summary, the proliferation of policy and practice in relation to family support services has led to a need for this project, involving both a mapping of provision and an exploration of current examples of good practice.

Methods

In this research project, a multi-methodological approach has been used (for further details see the Appendix). A literature review was conducted, building on previous comprehensive reviews undertaken by members of the research team (see for example, Mullender, 1996; Hague et al, 1996a; Parkinson and Humphreys, 1998; Hester et al, 1998/2000). The research design was divided into two stages: stage one consisted of a national mapping survey of provision; stage two consisted of in-depth case studies. Throughout the project, data from the literature review, the questionnaires and the case studies were used to develop and elaborate a framework of good practice indicators.

The study was conducted at the same time as research on accommodation and support for households experiencing domestic violence was in progress, supported by the Department of the Environment, Transport and the Regions (DETR), the DoH and the Women's Unit; the findings from the latter study will be available in the autumn of 2000. The two projects worked alongside each other and this report draws on some of the data collected by WAFE on behalf of the DETR, DoH and the Women's Unit as part of the above research project. Any conclusions drawn by the authors of this report are not necessarily endorsed by the government departments concerned however.

Mapping of domestic violence family support provision

This section contains information on the following:

- Women's Aid and women's refuge, outreach and advocacy services;
- the children's charities – Barnardo's, The Children's Society, NCH Action for Children and the NSPCC;
- statutory social services and social work departments, and health and social service trusts;
- perpetrators' programmes.

Women's Aid and women's refuge, outreach and advocacy services – mapping data

Women's refuge, outreach and advocacy services were surveyed with the cooperation of WAFE, using a questionnaire which they had developed for use in wider surveys, including those conducted for the DETR. Responses to this questionnaire were coordinated by Women's Aid in England through an individual telephone interview with each project in England. The research team similarly surveyed refuges in Scotland, Wales and Northern Ireland. An almost 100% response rate was obtained, with questionnaires completed for a total of 326 refuge projects.

The questionnaire elicited information (mainly quantitative in nature) about refuge services, about outreach, aftercare and advice services, and about training, consultancy and public education work. These data were supplemented by consultation with key officers, and by an analysis of policy and practice documents and guidance (see the Appendix for details).

General provision of services

As the key national agency representing abused women and their children, Women's Aid provides refuge, support and outreach services throughout the UK. These services are coordinated through the four Women's Aid federations: Northern Ireland Women's Aid, Scottish Women's Aid, Welsh Women's Aid and the Women's Aid Federation of England. Some specialist provision has been established for black women and women from minority ethnic communities, including a network of Asian women's refuges, although general refuges are, of course, open to all women. The point of establishing specialist refuges is to offer women who are members of particular ethnic communities or special groups a choice of which provision they would prefer to use. A very limited number of other specialist refuges exists, for example, for women without children, for those who have been sexually abused or for women who have learning disabilities. Although a member of Women's Aid, Refuge operates its own provision, and some other refuges also exist outside the Women's Aid network. The latter include those provided directly by some housing associations and some specialist refuges for black women (all of which were included in the study).

Refuges emerged in the 1970s and 1980s, were loosely connected to the women's movement and have always had principles emphasising the value of mutual support and the central importance of building on the views of abused women and children (see for example, Dobash and Dobash, 1992). An analysis of their current documentation reveals that these principles have endured, although few refuges now operate completely as collectives, as they did originally. Rather, refuges now have management committees and (sometimes complicated) staff teams. WAFE works towards the following principles:

- to believe women and children and to make their safety a priority;
- to support and empower women to take control of their own lives;
- to recognise and care for the needs of children affected by violence;
- to promote equal opportunities and anti-discriminatory practice.

The federations are served by a staff of national officers. These officers provide management and development services to refuges and outreach projects; produce directories, briefing papers and many other publications; lobby for relevant policy and legislative changes; provide advice and public education; and deliver training and consultancy. Self-help, self-determination and empowerment for women and children form important foundation stones underlying all their work.

The data revealed that refuges offer a wide range of support and advocacy services, as well as safe, emergency refuge accommodation. Where possible, aftercare and specialist children's services are provided, and there has been an increasing development of outreach projects in recent years. Local telephone advice lines are operated by individual projects throughout the country, and all refuge groups in Northern Ireland run their own advice centres. A National Domestic Violence Helpline is provided by WAFE; other helplines are run by the Refuge organisation in London and by Northern Ireland Women's Aid (covering the Northern Ireland area).

Partnership and joint inter-agency working

The questionnaire responses showed that women's refuge and outreach services engage in many partnerships with other agencies in different localities. Data from the study revealed a number of 'one-off', joint projects between Women's Aid and, variously, the NSPCC and other children's charities, social services, local black women's projects, mental health organisations, community development groups, and so on. Overall, about 80% (n=260) of refuge projects participated in multi-agency domestic violence forums, and the questionnaires recorded a large number of sub-groups of forums, and publications produced – with Women's Aid input – as a result. For instance, in many areas, inter-agency work with

schools and education departments had resulted in the production of education packs. Other examples included setting up children's and young people's forums, joint work between Women's Aid, inter-agency forums and ACPCs, participation in crime and disorder partnerships and so forth.

Underfunding

While lack of resources affects many agencies, including the children's charities, there is some agreement throughout the field that refuge groups are particularly underfunded. Such underfunding emerged in this study, as it has in many others (for example, Ball, 1995; Hague et al, 1996a), as a critical factor affecting the provision of service and the capacity of Women's Aid to engage in joint partnerships. For example, in this study, 12% (n=29) of English refuge groups and 14% (n=10) of refuge groups in the rest of the UK reported that they were unable to provide any children's services due to lack of funding; 42% (n=106) and 60% (n=44), respectively, were dependent on volunteers to keep their children's programmes going (even where paid childcare posts existed) (see also Hague et al, 1996a, for an analysis of children's work in refuges). These figures should be viewed in light of the fact that children are the majority of refuge residents, and are often facing a personal situation of severe trauma. (We recognise that the government has acknowledged this need, for instance, through the consultation document *Supporting people: A new policy and funding framework for support services* [DSS, 1998], although the longer-term proposals will not be implemented until 2003. See also Women's Unit of the Cabinet Office and Home Office, 1999.)

Details of provision

The following figures were derived from the survey. The Women's Aid Federation of England has 350 members, including both groups and individuals. It accommodated 54,500 women and children in 1998/99 and assisted a further 145,000, with an additional 21,000 calls to the National Domestic Violence Helpline. Northern Ireland Women's Aid operated 14 refuges through 11 groups accommodating 2,985 women and children, and providing information and advice to a further 17,713 women, including 8,000 calls to the helpline. With 33 member refuge groups (42 refuges in all), Welsh Women's Aid accommodated 5,350 women and children, offered outreach and support to a further 3,350 and telephone advice to 16,245. Scottish Women's Aid has 38 refuge groups offering 325 bed spaces. In the 1999 figures, 2,856 women and 3,943 children were accommodated and 50,971 contacts were made (both by telephone and in person) for information and support. In all, 69,634 women and children throughout the UK were provided with accommodation, and more than a quarter of a million (n=262,279) women used outreach and helpline services (note: this figure will include women who made contact on more than one occasion).

Services for women

Table 1 shows some examples of services offered to women using refuge and outreach projects.

Refuge groups also offered specific support to survivors of sexual abuse, lesbians, women with no recourse to public funds, women who are HIV positive, and so on. Of the refuge groups studied, 79% (n=253) provided clothing and personal items; 70% (n=228) provided a service to remove and reclaim possessions; 78% (n=248) provided

support with childcare and family welfare. Other services described in the study included 24-hour cover, on-call services, training for women service users, support with court dealings, health problems or immigration issues, arranging contact with fathers, and assertiveness and confidence building.

A variety of services were offered to black women and children by specialist refuges, but also by many generalist refuges. These included black women's support groups, translation and interpreting, attention to dietary needs, special children's programmes, information on community links, provision for religious observance and specialist African-Caribbean, Asian, Chinese and other staff (see WAFE, 1999b).

A similar variety of services were offered to disabled women (see Table 2), although at a much lower rate and, in general, access and facilities could be greatly improved.

Signing services were provided by 21% (n=53) of English refuges and 14% (n=10) of refuges in Scotland, Wales and Northern Ireland, with much smaller percentages offering other services, such

Table 1: Women using Women's Aid refuge and outreach projects (%)

	WAFE (N=250)	Welsh, Scottish and Northern Ireland Women's Aids (N=76)
Individual one-to-one support	90	99
Women's support groups	45	56
One-to-one counselling	42	35
Confidentiality/safety measures	90	97
Support and advocacy (housing/legal and so on)	90	99
Legal advice/information	90	97
Support with drug and alcohol dependency	46	63
Support with mental health problems	53	71

Table 2: Women's Aid services catering for women with disabilities (%)

	WAFE (N=250)	Welsh, Scottish and Northern Ireland Women's Aids (N=76)
Accessible general premises	26	32
Accessible premises for outreach services	13	23
Links with local disabled people's organisations	39	23

as Braille, induction loops, minicoms and so on (only between 1% and 4% in all cases).

Services for children

In the questionnaire data, 69% of English refuges and 89% in Wales, Scotland and Northern Ireland employed specialist children's workers (although a high percentage were part-time rather than full-time); 27% and 12%, respectively, employed sessional children's workers.

Table 3 shows some examples of services offered to children using refuge projects.

Of refuges in the UK, 12% of refuges in England and 4% of refuges elsewhere offer specific services to black children, indicating the greater number of specialist refuges within England; and a small number offer specific services divided by gender for either boys or girls. Some refuges also attempt to offer specific services for children with special needs, for example, for disabled children (but only approximately 5% overall).

More than 60% of refuges overall hold children's meetings, which frequently have decision-making power and can influence project running. Children's work in refuges usually utilises an empowerment model, believing in and raising children's views wherever possible and often engaging in imaginative work to deal with abuse.

Outreach services

The majority of refuge projects offer outreach and support services (71% in England; 88% in Wales, Scotland and Northern Ireland). In many cases, these are provided through a dedicated outreach project which may also provide aftercare for women and children who have moved on. Outreach services include one-to-one support, groups in the community, telephone support, advocacy with other organisations and educational activities.

Most refuge groups also offer advice – often through a specific advice centre/service. For England and for the rest of the UK, 56% and 93% of groups respectively have a 24-hour telephone service, and 16% and 81% respectively offer a separate advice service. In some cases, the latter includes advice sessions with solicitors, housing agencies and other specialists.

Training and practice guidance

Refuges and outreach groups engage in substantial training provision for outside agencies and also participate in a range of internal training. Good practice guidance documents have been developed widely and WAFE provides a national Domestic Violence Services Team to advise groups on practice, management and development issues. Further details on training and practice guidance offered are in Chapter 3 of this report.

Table 3: Services provided to children using Women's Aid refuges (%)

	WAFE (N=250)	Welsh, Scottish and Northern Ireland Women's Aids (N=76)
One-to-one support	64	81
One-to-one counselling	24	26
Groups – pre-school	72	89
Groups – school-age	69	89
Youthwork – older children	39	71
Children's advocacy	72	86
Children's welcome packs	46	75
After-school club	34	15
Holiday play schemes	46	52
Family holidays	22	27
Educational activities	44	48

Monitoring and evaluation

The data revealed that refuges are not systematically evaluated. Few refuge groups are in a financial position comprehensively to do this, although some joint projects with other agencies have been evaluated. Almost all refuges now monitor their referral rates and provision, and collect other data to meet grant requirements. According to study consultations, stringent monitoring conditions have been placed on refuge groups by some housing associations and local authorities, which take a disproportionate amount of time to meet in relation to the high pressures on staff working time available.

In conclusion

Our survey revealed a large array of services offered either by refuge and outreach services alone or in partnership with other agencies. However, these services were generally not thought to be adequate to meet the level of need, and it appeared that all refuges fell far short of being able to accommodate all the families who approached them. The responses to the questionnaire also demonstrate the previously noted fact that refuge groups in England are substantially less well funded than those in Scotland, Wales and Northern Ireland (which deal primarily with their own devolved governments).

Children's organisations – mapping data

It has to be recognised and acknowledged that, apart from Women's Aid, the other agencies surveyed in this study are not primarily concerned with support work for domestic violence, and domestic violence may not be their main focus.

A specific questionnaire was compiled to map the provision of support services by the major children's charities for families where there is domestic violence. The questionnaire was distributed by Barnardo's, The Children's Society, the NSPCC and NCH Action for Children to all their constituent projects and a total of 449 projects returned the questionnaire – an overall return rate of 59.5% (see the Appendix for details).

Provision of services

The children's charities were engaged in a tremendous variety of activities, including child protection investigations, recovery work with children following abuse, specific support for children with disabilities, help with accommodation and housing, arrangement of fostering and adoption, and involvement in family mediation. While domestic violence may be of relevance to any work with children, understanding of its relevance appeared to depend on the type of activity that projects were engaged in – those carrying out child protection investigations were most likely to consider domestic violence as an issue for the children concerned. The projects engaged in family mediation were also, as a result of their screening policy, especially aware of domestic violence as a potential issue (see Hester et al, 1997). Projects working with disabled children, or engaged in fostering and adoption, appeared least likely to see domestic violence as relevant to their work. One adoption project commented that adoptive parents would risk losing the child if they revealed domestic violence, yet the project did not seek such information despite the possible risk to the child.

Overall, the children's charities had a wide range of provision where families experiencing domestic violence might also receive support. This included a small number (n=6, 1.3%) of dedicated projects dealing specifically with women, children and/or men from families where there is domestic violence; a large number of projects (n=332, 73.9%) which were not set up to deal with domestic violence, but where the issue was nonetheless considered of relevance to service users and dealt with in the projects concerned; and a residuum of about a fifth of projects (n=87, 19.4%) where domestic violence was not considered an issue for the service users concerned (see Table 4). Some of the latter projects mentioned that their service users might have had experience of domestic violence but that such experience was no longer relevant, for instance once a child had been removed from the violent context. Clearly, there was a need for these projects to rethink the implications of such issues to their work, in particular the evidence of post-separation violence and the longer-term impacts on children and women of living with domestic violence (Hester et al, 1998/2000).

Table 4: Provision by children's charities of services for families experiencing domestic violence (% of all UK projects*)

Services provided by projects	
Specific	1.3
Integrated	73.9
None	19.4
	(N=449)

Note: * Percentages add to less than 100% as the remainder are missing data.

Table 5: People worked with by the children's charities (% of all UK projects*)

People worked with	
Children/young people	60.1
Children and mothers	53.5
Women	47.0
Children and carers	32.1
Men	22.5

Note: * Percentages add to more than 100% because projects may carry out more than one category of work.

> "We are a youth homelessness project and inevitably many of the young people we come into contact with have either experienced and/ or witnessed domestic abuse. Our primary concern is their housing safety, but we do try and have a holistic approach to the needs of young people." (Children's Society project)

Altogether 20 projects said they had either a designated domestic violence worker, or someone from the project was deemed especially knowledgeable, and/or they used a freelance domestic violence worker. A further project had attempted to establish a specific post, but had been unsuccessful in their bid to fund this.

As would be expected of children's organisations, most of the direct work carried out in relation to domestic violence involved children and young people (n=270, 60.1%). Over half of the projects also worked with children and mothers together (n=240, 53.5%), children and their carers (n=144, 32.1%), or women on their own (n=211, 47.0%); men were worked with by over a fifth of the projects surveyed (n=101, 22.5%) (see Table 5).

Agencies often provided more than one type of service where families experiencing domestic violence might be supported. For children, these included one-to-one support, advocacy with other agencies and groupwork. For both women and men, services also included one-to-one support and advocacy with other agencies, with financial and practical help the third largest type for women and drop-in sessions the third largest type

for men. Other services included crèche/childcare provision and mediation (see Table 6). Respondents identified a particular need for more direct and ongoing work with children, as well as other support work for children, and preventative work with both children and adults.

In the commentary, a number of projects mentioned child contact and work they were doing with children resulting from difficult child contact arrangements, involvement in contact negotiations, handover or contact supervision involving domestic violence.

An NCH project explained:

> "Women's Aid are now using our premises to encourage access and handover visits between partners of children where domestic violence has been an issue."

Differences between services in rural and urban areas were also mentioned, with one project suggesting that, for them, the most effective way of working with domestic violence issues in a rural area was to set up regular women's groups with a crèche attached and possibly transport laid on.

For just over a fifth of the projects, domestic violence services were accessed by adults and children from a range of cultural or ethnic minority backgrounds (n=103, 22.9%), and a quarter were accessed by adults or children with disabilities (n=115, 25.6%).

Table 6: Types of services provided by the children's charities (% of all UK projects)

Service provided	For children	For women	For men
One-to-one support	40.8	42.1	11.4
Advocacy	29.2	35.0	8.7
Groupwork	14.3	16.7	3.1
Drop-in sessions	13.1	16.3	4.9
Financial and/or practical help	11.6	17.1	4.5
Safe accommodation	3.8	2.9	1.6
Other	10.2	8.9	4.2

Table 7: Indirect services provided by the children's charities (% of all UK projects)

Indirect service provided	For children	For women	For men
Publications and leaflets	20.3	34.5	14.0
Community-based approach	17.1	20.3	7.1
Telephone	7.8	9.6	4.2
Information packs	5.8	11.1	3.6
Other	8.5	9.4	5.1

As well as the direct services outlined above, projects were engaged in providing indirect advice and information services for people in situations of domestic violence aimed at women, in particular. These largely involved making publications and leaflets about domestic violence available to service users; a small number of projects also provided telephone support lines for women, children or men (see Table 7).

In addition, a small number of projects provided public education and training with regard to domestic violence (n=80, 17.8%)

Screening

Only a few projects routinely asked about domestic violence – most found out from a combination of service users themselves and/or referring agencies or individuals stating that domestic violence was an issue (see Table 8).

Table 8: How children's charities identify domestic violence as an issue (% of all UK projects*)

Domestic violence identified by...	
Service users and referrers	49.7
Service user statement	20.7
Referrer	4.5
Always asking	2.9
All combined	11.6

Note: * Percentages add to less than 100% because not all projects saw the question as relevant.

One project had established its own research group consisting of young people, to ascertain young people's views and needs concerning domestic violence. The results from the Rotherham Young People's Domestic Violence Research Group survey, based on questionnaire and focus group data, were being used by The Children's Society as the basis for developing services and support relating to domestic violence for young people in Rotherham. With regard to seeking help, young people identified the education services – in particular teachers – as the first person they would go to, more that any other professional individual. Youthworkers, the police, social workers, health workers, counsellors, workers from voluntary organisations and religious leaders were also identified. Informal help and support were identified as being available through friends, relatives and family members.

Those seen as able to provide a direct service to young people living with and experiencing domestic violence were predominantly national helplines and ChildLine, youthworkers, social services, the police, doctors, counsellors and children's charities. The young people consulted identified a wide range of potential services and support, which they thought should be made available to them. These included: support and accommodation to assist leaving home, confidential counselling, someone to talk to, local helplines, safe places to go specifically for children and young people, family support, education and awareness-raising in schools and the wider community, more widely available information, education about parenting, work with perpetrators to stop domestic violence, support groups and peer support.

Referrals and agency links

Almost half of the projects received specific referrals involving domestic violence (45.2%), mostly from social services. A small number of these referrals were received from the health services, from Women's Aid and other refuges, and from the police. Schools were the least likely to refer individuals to the children's organisations, despite young people themselves saying that they would be most likely to confide in teachers (McGee, 2000).

The vast majority of the projects surveyed – whether providing domestic violence services or not – were also likely to refer service users to other agencies where issues of domestic violence were concerned (81.3%). Social services were most likely to be referred to, followed by Women's Aid and other refuge providers; a lesser number of referrals were also made to the police and health services.

Forty-one per cent of the projects were involved in inter-agency forums and over a third of local ACPCs were thought to deal with domestic violence issues (38.1%), although a similar number of respondents did not know whether their local ACPC did or did not deal with such issues (34.1%).

One NSPCC project commented that:

"In our experience of working with Women's Aid for four years, we have a range of experience of the impact of domestic violence on families and children – including the murder of a survivor who was contracted to work with this agency."

Safety

Being safe is a prominent concern of women and children experiencing domestic violence. Projects were asked if they had specific policies and strategies to create safety plans for individuals where domestic violence was involved. Despite this emphasis, the replies concerned safety measures generally and not safety planning specifically, indicating a lack of knowledge about safety planning as a particular 'good practice' approach. Just over a fifth of projects had safety measures in relation to children, just under a fifth in relation to women, and less than half that number in relation to men's programmes (see Table 9). Overall, safety planning appeared somewhat ad hoc, with a need for greater clarity concerning the use of safety measures and in particular safety planning. The survey also indicates the need for individual, rather than merely institutional, safety planning to be carried out with both children and women.

Table 9: Personal safety provision by the children's charities (% of all UK projects*)

Safety policies and strategies	
For children	22.5
For women	18.5
In relation to men	8.0

Note: * Percentages add to less than 100% as not all projects have safety provision.

A much larger proportion of the projects had safety measures in place for workers (43.7%).

Training

Despite the large number of projects which were dealing in some way with domestic violence, only a small number of projects provided training on domestic violence issues for all paid staff and volunteers, with about a third of projects providing training to some staff. Training, where provided, was mainly of one or two days' duration, with a small number of projects also providing regular updating (see Table 10).

Table 10: Training on domestic violence issues provided by the children's charities (% of all UK projects*)

Participants	
All workers	15.8
Some workers	32.3

Duration	
Of one day or less	26.3
Of two days	10.0
Of more than two days	4.5
Training updated regularly	12.0

Note: * Percentages add to less than 100% as not all projects provided training.

Policies

Few projects said that they had guidelines, procedures or good practice statements regarding domestic violence (15.6%). Where such guidelines were deemed to exist they ranged from locally produced statements to use of nationally provided policy guidance. Given the existence of national guidelines and/or good practice statements for most of the children's charities surveyed, the apparent lack of local knowledge of these is somewhat surprising.

Monitoring and evaluation

Domestic violence was systematically monitored or recorded in only a fifth of projects (19.6%). The work carried out with people experiencing domestic violence was nonetheless evaluated in about a quarter of projects (26.7%), probably as part of a more general remit regarding evaluation of the projects' work.

In conclusion

The vast majority of the children's organisations surveyed come across domestic violence in their support work with families and many have developed ways of working with the resultant issues as a part of their general remit. Yet very few services are specifically aimed at supporting families experiencing domestic violence or have staff designated to deal with these issues. Domestic violence tends not to be screened for or monitored, and policy development is lacking in many local services. While safety of staff is taken into consideration by nearly half of the services, there is a need to further develop safety measures with regard to service users.

Social services departments: statutory sector – mapping data

A questionnaire was designed to map the services provided for families where there is domestic violence, as well as to gather other information about the policies and practices of social services departments in England and Wales and health and social services trusts in Northern Ireland (see Appendix A for details). Secondary sources (Henderson, 1997; Scottish Office, 1998; Zero Tolerance Charitable Trust, 1998) were used to ascertain the situation in Scotland as an audit of provision had only recently been undertaken.

We received a similar response rate from the questionnaires distributed in Northern Ireland (59%, n=10) and England/Wales (62%, n=104). While a direct comparison between countries was not possible (as Northern Ireland has developed a different structure for responding to domestic violence through joint health and social services trusts), it was nevertheless considered useful to lay out selected data from each country and to note where there were differences in the development of services.

Provision of services

Social services departments nationally see very high numbers of children, women and men who are living in situations of domestic violence. However, for the purposes of the mapping exercise, we were interested in the development of services and organisational policies rather than the general work of individual practitioners. The questionnaire divided service provision into two

main categories: specific support services and integrated support services. Specific services were defined as projects that have a primary focus on domestic violence (such as a long-term team established to undertake recovery work with children who have lived with domestic violence). Integrated services were defined as other projects that address the issue of domestic violence in a significant way, but not as the primary focus of the service (such as a family centre where there is a support group for women in situations of domestic violence).

While considerable service development in the area has occurred, it is of concern that, in England and Wales, at least one fifth of social services departments have no special provision, either directly or through service level agreements, for families where there is domestic violence. In part, this might have been compensated for by other departments providing services (such as the housing department providing refuge funding). The Northern Ireland health and social services trusts were found to operate higher numbers of support services and had services available in all geographic areas that responded.

Table 11: Service provision in social services departments in England, Wales and Northern Ireland

Services provided	England and Wales		Northern Ireland	
	n	%	n	%
Specific and integrated	33	34	6	60
Specific only	19	19	2	20
Integrated only	26	27	2	20
No services available	20	20	0	0
Total responses	98		10	

West Sussex Council

In West Sussex, a variety of services are run or supported by social services departments. In Worthing, the social services department is involved in the running of a drop-in group for women experiencing, or who have experienced, domestic violence, in conjunction with Worthing Women's Aid and a crèche provided by the local Mothers' Union.

Financial support is given to Crawley Women's Aid, and Crawley NSPCC has a service level agreement to provide a group for children aged between six and nine who have experienced domestic violence, which is run in conjunction with a group for parents and carers. There is also an agreement between Crawley NSPCC, Crawley Family Centre, and Crawley Women's Aid to provide groupwork for children, and individual and/or groupwork with women who are resident in the refuge. Crawley Social Services are also involved in a pilot partnership project with Crawley Probation Service to provide a support service for the partners of men attending a perpetrators' group.

Table 12: Types of service provision provided through social services departments*

Services provided	England and Wales		Northern Ireland	
	n	%	n	%
Safe accommodation	43	41	7	70
One-to-one support/counselling	40	38	8	80
Contact support	20	19	3	30
Group sessions	29	28	4	40
Advocacy	29	28	7	70
Drop-in sessions	26	25	5	50
Other	14	13	3	30
Total responses	98		10	

Note: * Percentages total greater than 100% as each box represents the percentage of respondents providing each service.

Throughout the UK, many of the services mentioned above are provided through service level agreements. This reflects the increasing trend towards social services as a purchaser rather than provider of services. For instance, in Scotland, 85% of social work departments provide funding for domestic violence organisations (mainly Women's Aid) but did not have budgets for providing their own direct service (Henderson, 1997). In England and Wales, a similar proportion (14%) of the specific services were directly provided by the social services department.

Many examples of the diverse ways in which service provision occurs were given in the questionnaire responses.

Table 12 gives a breakdown of the types of specific support services provided or funded by social services. It does not include integrated support services, and it should also be recognised that some provisions are supported through funding by other departments within the local authority.

Children's Services Plans

One indicator of provision is available through Children's Services Plans (CSPs). These multi-agency plans should reflect the development of services for 'children in need'. Table 13 shows a disparity between how domestic violence is recorded within CSPs and the actual levels of

Table 13: Children's Services Plans, levels of awareness and service provision*

Entry in Children's Services Plans	England and Wales		Northern Ireland	
	n	%	n	%
Domestic violence mentioned in CSPs	72	71	5	50
Domestic violence mentioned, but no provisions made	19	18	3	30
Domestic violence service provision made as part of CSP	21	20	1	10
Provision for staff training made	29	28	2	20
Total responses	101		10	

Note: * Percentages total greater than 100% as answers were not mutually exclusive.

service provision, which is far lower. Although Northern Ireland has higher levels of service provision shown in one part of our questionnaire, this was not reflected in its CSPs. This possibly reflects a lack of 'joined-up' thinking between different parts of a multi-agency forum and the health and social services planning sections.

A significant number of local authorities do recognise and mention the issue of children living with domestic violence; however, this translates, at this stage, into only a minority of local authorities actually providing support services for children in need. A similar picture emerged in Scotland (Scottish Women's Aid, 2000) where three quarters of the 32 local authorities recognise the emotional effects of domestic violence on children and young people and define them as 'children in need'. However, the study concluded that the majority of councils would address the major gaps in services for these children through developing a multi-agency approach ('within resources'), rather than committing themselves to specific targets for provision of services.

Social services and domestic violence forums

A positive finding of the research is the extent of social services departments' involvement in local domestic violence forums. Most authorities have recognised the need for multi-agency working in the area of domestic violence. The further step recommended by the 1995 inter-agency circular (Home Office and Welsh Office, 1995) – to have a representative from the domestic violence forum as a member of the ACPC – has been taken by approximately half of the local authorities in England and Wales and 70% in Northern Ireland.

Specialist domestic violence workers

Throughout England and Wales, 46% of social services departments have a designated person responsible for either domestic violence policy or practice development; 12% of these workers have no work relief associated with the position and therefore carry the domestic violence work on top of their normal duties. One third of the remaining social services departments contribute funds to either a full or part-time specialist domestic violence worker or domestic violence forum coordinator. Without designated workers policy development is difficult – 46% of social services departments had not yet developed policies and guidelines for domestic violence.

Coventry City Council

The social services department of Coventry City Council (1999) has provided joint funding for a full-time post responsible for increasing multi-agency cooperation and producing a strategy which will ensure a consistent city-wide response to the needs of women and children experiencing domestic violence. The Domestic Violence Liaison Officer works for the Domestic Violence Focus Group and takes a proactive approach in encouraging a corporate strategy. This strategy has elicited pledges and action plans from a wide range of statutory and voluntary organisations to improve the responses to domestic violence by individual agencies and inter-agency coordination.

Table 14: Domestic violence (DV) forums*

	England and Wales		Northern Ireland	
	Number	%	Number	%
DV forum in the area	97	93	10	100
Designated liaison from social services department to DV forum	93	89	9	90
DV forum representative on ACPC	51	49	7	70
Total responses	104		10	

Note: * Answers were not mutually exclusive and therefore total more than 100%.

In Northern Ireland, half of the health and social services trusts pay for either a full-time or part-time specialist domestic violence worker or domestic violence forum coordinator, and 60% of the health and social services trusts have a designated domestic violence worker.

An innovative model for designated workers is provided by Newham Social Services Department.

Case study: Newham Social Services

Newham Social Services Department core funds eight domestic violence advisors – four based in social services and four based in the voluntary sector. These positions are in addition to standard refuge provision. The role of the team is to provide:

- direct work with women in situations of domestic violence;
- consultation to social workers on issues of domestic violence;
- awareness raising and training regarding domestic violence within the borough/local community.

Social services also jointly funds, with the Metropolitan Police, a pilot community partnership project to coordinate support services to women fleeing domestic violence who contact the police.

The employment of domestic violence advisors situated within social services recognises the difficulties experienced by social workers involved in child protection in focusing on the needs of the woman experiencing domestic violence. The strength of this model of working lies in its acknowledgement of a number of issues:

- at times there may be a conflict of interest between the woman and the child(ren);
- attending to the needs of the mother may be the most effective means of supporting and protecting children;
- social workers frequently have not been trained to attend to the issues of domestic violence and accessible consultation from a specialist team potentially overcomes this gap in skills and knowledge;
- women are often concerned about contacting social services departments for help; however, the high rates of self-referral to the Domestic Violence Team within social services in Newham suggests that this strategy is working to increase women's ability to seek help and the ability of social services to offer appropriate and accessible family support.

A further strength of the team lies in its ethnic diversity and the range of languages spoken by the advisors. The innovative work of the team has yet to be independently evaluated.

Table 15: Staff training provided by social services departments

Training offered by departments/trusts	England and Wales		Northern Ireland	
	n	%	n	%
No training on domestic violence	36	31.5	0	0
Basic training*	70	74	8	89
Specialist training*	71	75	8	89
Total responses	95		9	

Note: * Answers in the second and third rows were not mutually exclusive and therefore total more than 100%.

Staff training

The mix of training provided for staff varies considerably in both the range of courses on offer and the numbers of staff attending. Some local authorities only provide basic training or awareness-raising sessions, while others provide basic training as well as more specialist training, or solely specialist training (for example on 'domestic violence and the law', or 'assessment issues and domestic violence'). Table 15 also shows that some areas still offer no training.

In recognition of the significance of training, the DoH commissioned the development of a training pack and reader to resource this area – *Making an impact: Children and domestic violence* (Barnardo's et al, 1998; Hester et al, 1998/2000). The recent DoH questionnaire to social services departments (DoH, 1999b) showed that while almost 70% (n=64) of their sample (N=92) had attended the DoH regional dissemination workshops on the training pack, 55% (n=51) had not taken domestic violence training forward using the pack, although a further 14 of these had plans to do so.

Screening for domestic violence

There is encouraging evidence from the survey that the practice of enquiring about domestic violence is increasing (see Table 16), although, in England and Wales, this still does not occur in over half of social services departments. Furthermore, even in areas where questions about domestic violence are routinely asked, this information is not systematically recorded or used as a basis for future planning. In total, 85% of social services departments in England and Wales have not introduced systems for routinely screening, recording or collating information relating to domestic violence.

Although in Northern Ireland it is encouraging to see that 70% of trusts who responded have introduced routine screening, 90% still have not introduced systems for recording the information. In Scotland, three social work departments collated statistics or information in relation to domestic violence, although this was not undertaken in a routine way.

Table 16: Domestic violence screening rates in social services departments*

	England and Wales		Northern Ireland	
	Number	%	Number	%
Routine screening for domestic violence	48	47	7	70
Results recorded and collated	15	15	1	10
Total responses	103		10	

Note: * Each row represents a separate question and therefore columns do not aggregate to 100%.

In conclusion

The mapping of domestic violence provision through social services departments shows that significant steps have been taken to improve services, as well as the infrastructure to recognise and respond to domestic violence. However, a criticism remains that provision is geographically patchy – although some areas of the UK provide a comprehensive range of services, in other localities there are no designated domestic violence services provided through the social services departments. Children's Services Plans frequently recognise children in situations of domestic violence as children in need, although many areas have yet to find the resources to respond with service provision to this group of children. A minority of social services departments routinely screen and monitor for domestic violence during child protection investigations. While domestic violence awareness training is now a priority for many social services departments, provision is very varied, with some areas failing to offer any training at all. Although the numbers of social services departments participating in domestic violence forums was encouraging, many areas do not have a designated member of staff responsible for policies or practice in relation to domestic violence.

Perpetrators' programmes – mapping data

Although it makes sense to report this work separately because it is very different from that discussed in the other sections of this chapter, the researchers recognise that perpetrators' programmes represent only a small proportion of the questionnaires returned for the total project and also only constitute a small element of total provision.

Introduction

Intervention with perpetrators requires men to take responsibility for their abusive behaviour. It is also unusual among the types of intervention documented in this study in having a national statement of good practice (RESPECT, 2000) and a large body of effectiveness research (summarised in Mullender and Burton, 2000).

Nevertheless, it remains a controversial area of practice. There are fears that, if inappropriately conducted, it may divert abusers from facing full legal consequences; offer false hope to partners; teach perpetrators more subtle ways to intimidate; compete for funding with services for women and children; and be unaccountable to survivors. overall its effectiveness is far from proven (Mullender, 1996). Certainly, the survey revealed a number of areas in which care should be exercised in setting up any new project.

Methodology and response rate

A mapping of perpetrators' programmes was conducted by questionnaire survey of National Practitioners' Network (NPN) members (backed up by attendance at the spring 1999 NPN meeting) and of all 91 UK probation services. (NPN has now developed into RESPECT: The National Association for Domestic Violence Perpetrator Programmes and Associated Support Services.) Twenty-six responses were obtained about services being offered: six from the voluntary sector and 20 probation services (of the latter, seven reported partnership arrangements for the main or a complementary service, such as work with partners). While non-response may or may not equate with lack of involvement and high turnover makes it difficult to keep track of initiatives, this response rate compares favourably with the NPN directory and with other surveys (Mullender, 1996; Scourfield and Dobash, 1999).

Nineteen of the respondents were involved in specialist provision for perpetrators, including or solely based on groups in 18 cases.

Policy and good practice

Eleven respondents to the mapping survey said their own agencies had specific policies on domestic violence and the same number had practice guidelines; eight had specific procedures; eleven were party to a wider domestic violence strategy, for example, through a local forum. Worryingly, five were clear that there was no policy in place in their agency.

Form of attendance and selection criteria

The survey showed a typical mix of voluntary and court-mandated attenders, with the proportion of the latter in probation-run groups ranging from 5% to 100%. Two voluntary sector and six probation groups had only mandated members; another four of the latter had 90% or more.

Of the 19 active projects responding, nine stated that they took all referrals; the 10 operating selection criteria were principally seeking a degree of motivation. Other concerns were alcohol or drug misuse and mental health problems, although far more groups took men with these multiple problems than refused them. Several stressed that such factors are not the cause of the violence.

Models of intervention

The move towards regarding domestic violence perpetrators as responsible for their criminal behaviour has been mirrored in a shift to a cognitive–behavioural rather than a psychotherapeutic approach and in a degree of uniformity between perpetrators' programmes both here and overseas (Tolman and Edleson, 1995; Scourfield and Dobash, 1999). Most groups in the study were based on a social learning, that is, a broadly behavioural approach.

Adding a gender analysis typically leads to a combined model similar to that pioneered in Duluth (Pence and Paymar, 1996) – all but one of the detailed responses referred to Duluth as a major influence. In terms of source publications, nine respondents had gleaned their knowledge from the CHANGE manual (Morran and Wilson, 1997), itself influenced by Duluth. The most common self-description by projects was 'educational', with 16 giving this as a total or combined description; 15 groups said their main aim was increasing women and children's safety, 13 that they existed to challenge or change men's attitudes to violence, and 11 to reduce the risk of re-offending. RESPECT holds to the principle that: "The primary aim in working with perpetrators of domestic violence is to increase the safety of women and children" (2000, p 7), and this has been endorsed as good practice by central government (Women's Unit of the Cabinet Office and Home Office, 1999, p 38).

In order to explore the underpinnings of the approach and aims selected, respondents were asked: "Can you briefly describe how your organisation understands why men are violent?". Thirteen wrote something about men's power and control, while five cited social learning about attitudes to women.

Women's safety

All 19 active respondents limited men's rights to confidentiality so that partners could be given information about progress, and about any risks to their or their children's safety, either directly or through a partners' programme where one existed. Typically, the supervising probation officer of mandated men was also informed, and police and social services would be told of any disclosure of child abuse. However, one of the voluntary sector projects would check with the man before revealing anything, even though it was among those requiring the man to sign a consent form allowing information about him to be passed on to other agencies.

Contact with women was routine, with all 19 active respondents having direct links with support services for women, 15 running their own linked partner support and all providing information about relevant services for women and children. Almost all provided partners with help on safety planning, legal information, and details of programme content – notably the emphasis on men's, not women's, responsibility. All groups claimed to discourage unrealistic expectations of men's attendance and to avoid competing directly for funds with women's domestic violence services, although only eight had this last point as written policy.

Worryingly, seven projects surveyed had no child protection policies, four had not given women's organisations a voice in programme design and delivery, three did not keep partners informed if men failed to attend and two did not tell partners if men were asked to leave. This could potentially result in women and children being placed in renewed danger. One groupwork programme was not seeking confidential feedback from partners about men's current behaviour, which would leave it unable to conduct a valid evaluation (Mullender and Burton, 2000).

Duration

RESPECT's (2000) minimum standard if programme duration is at least 75 hours over a minimum of 30 weeks. Groups listed by survey respondents ranged from 20 hours over 10 weeks to 120 hours over 48 weeks, the latter supplemented by a further 12 hours of one-to-one work. The shortest of these clearly do not meet the recommended standard.

Non-completion rates

The international literature reveals problems in getting men through an entire programme (Gondolf, 1997, 1998a; NCAVAC, 1998). In the survey, only five groups claimed an 80-90% completion rate; three were as low as 30%, four did not know or did not reply, and the rest lay somewhere between a 50% and 75% completion rate. However, groups interpreted completion differently – six required full attendance, nine a defined proportion of attendances (for example, two absences condoned), one was still deciding and one did not reply; one left it to the individual's probation officer to decide whether an absence had been satisfactorily explained.

Penalties for non-completion also varied and revealed that not all local probation services or magistrates' benches were collaborating effectively with perpetrators' projects. Three respondents specifically stated that little would happen, with recommendations to breach not carried through or resentencing giving varying messages about seriousness. Some men were ordered to continue in the group and others not.

Size of groups

Groups set a ceiling of eight to 12 members (although five did not set a maximum), and were actually working with an average attendance from as low as four to as high as 15. Eight had a rolling membership, nine a closed membership, and two worked in two stages with one open and the other closed (although not in the same order in each case).

Programme facilitators

The norm (11/18) was for groups to have two facilitators; seven had three, one of which added a fourth person as consultant. All but one had a male–female partnership to model equality, mutual respect and joint conflict resolution, and to bring gendered viewpoints to discussions.

Five reported having full-time staff involved, the largest number being four and the others ranging from one to 2.5. Eight others had part-time staff, although three of these had from eight to 16 workers involved (the rest had from one to four, in at least one case on a sessional basis). Three projects cited designated practitioner posts, two in policy and one in practice.

Training

Although RESPECT emphasises adequate training, the survey found a varied picture. All but one of the projects reported that facilitators had had some basic awareness training on domestic violence, although eight had only attended one- or two-day courses (and several others did not specify). A majority (16), but by no means all, had had training specifically in working with perpetrators and this had typically lasted longer. However, four had had only a couple of days' preparation. Nor had all provided child protection training or any work on the safety issues affecting women and children.

Inter-agency involvement

All 19 respondents had a domestic violence forum in their area and all sent a designated liaison person to attend it. The forum was in turn represented on the management committees of three probation and three voluntary groups. One voluntary sector project had found the local Safer Communities Group to be more proactive than the forum and currently held the chair of this body.

There were additional specific links for at least half the projects with relevant local initiatives, mostly in the voluntary sector, ranging from a fathers' group to an NSPCC women and children's group. Other examples of good inter-agency work included a jointly funded partner support group, joint training for magistrates and links through the local Community Safety Strategy.

Wider influence

Several programmes had become involved in providing training and consultancy, or in public education. The range of materials produced included posters, leaflets, a video, information packs and educational materials including exercises and quizzes. A smaller number had published, either in journals or in manuals.

In conclusion

Respondents gave considerable evidence of having thought carefully about various aspects of their practice. There was less evidence of the groups' context being consistently supportive, either within their agencies, where training levels and screening varied enormously, or in the wider criminal justice system, where few programmes talked about clear or rigorous policies on breaching non-attenders.

However, there are certain things that we do know which can form the basis of best practice indicators. Notably, parallel work with women and building women's accounts into evaluation are crucial (Mullender and Burton, 2000; and see Chapter 3), as is seriously considering the safety of women and children in the way the group is conducted, and forging effective links with a range of local organisations – notably independent services for women and children.

3

Good practice indicators

The broad picture described in the preceding section was used by the research team as a basis from which to develop specific good practice indicators for domestic violence work. By 'good practice indicators' we mean specific developments which are essential to good practice, that should be aspired to, and which can be used as parameters in evaluations. The good practice indicators discussed below have been derived from an overview of the mapping survey results; from the range of definitions and documentation which were attached to many of the questionnaires; from the specific case studies which supplemented the general mapping data; and from previous research and practice – all informed by the two principles which have guided the study (see page 1). This process led to the formulation of eight good practice indicators. It should be noted, however, that this list of indicators may not be exhaustive and is likely to develop over time as new practice

emerges. The eight good practice indicators are listed below.

Under each of these broad good practice indicators, further sub-indicators of good practice are listed in this chapter. These indicators are of strategic value in terms of the management and development of domestic violence services, but each also includes practical, operational issues. The final indicator, which relates to the practical 'how-to' of specific work with women who have experienced domestic violence and their children, was developed mainly from the case studies and comprises a range of operational issues underlying best practice. In relation to work with perpetrators guidelines are available from RESPECT.

Good Practice Indicator 1:	The use of definitions of domestic violence
Good Practice Indicator 2:	The use of monitoring processes and screening
Good Practice Indicator 3:	Good practice guidelines and domestic violence policies
Good Practice Indicator 4:	Safety measures and safety-oriented practice
Good Practice Indicator 5:	Training
Good Practice Indicator 6:	Evaluation
Good Practice Indicator 7:	Multi-agency integration and coordination
Good Practice Indicator 8:	Specific working with women and children

Good Practice Indicator 1: Definitions – setting the parameters

Clarity about what is meant by the term domestic violence is undeniably important in designing and delivering services. However, arriving at agreed understandings and definitions of domestic violence for a project, organisation or inter-agency forum is a potentially contentious matter. Any term or definition will include, exclude, or emphasise, different aspects of the problem. The negotiation and adoption of a definition of domestic violence is an indicator that the issue has been discussed and agreed, and that the organisations concerned are able to make a clear statement about it. Without such a definition, other steps, such as monitoring and screening for domestic violence, are unlikely to occur. However, what such a definition should contain is a complex issue.

Sub-indicator: Definitions should acknowledge diversity and the gendered nature of domestic violence, and include different types of abuse

Definitions generally include a range of types of abusive behaviour (such as, physical, sexual, emotional, psychological, financial and so on). Some definitions are also gender-specific in their analysis of domestic violence; for example, WAFE includes the following in their definition:

> Domestic violence is the physical, sexual or psychological abuse of a person (usually a woman) with whom they have an intimate relationship. (WAFE, 1998)

Further details of violence follow in the definition, including sexual, emotional and mental violence as well as physical abuse. The Leeds Inter-agency Project has been unequivocal in always naming domestic violence as 'violence against women by known men', and a number of other areas and organisations have followed suit.

These definitions recognise that women are the primary targets of domestic violence. It is difficult for organisations with gender-specific definitions to agree to definitions in multi-agency forums and partnerships that do not recognise the gendered nature of domestic violence. However, various organisations in the study used gender-neutral definitions. For example, the Home Office definition (or a variation of it) which leaves out gender was frequently used, either as the full definition or as a starting point for domestic violence policy documents. The emphasis here is on a range of abusive behaviours:

> Domestic violence includes any form of physical, sexual or emotional abuse between people in a close relationship. It can take a number of forms such as physical assault, sexual abuse, rape, threats and intimidation. It may also be accompanied by other kinds of intimidation such as degradation, mental and verbal abuse, humiliation and systematic criticism. (Home Office and Welsh Office, 1995)

A possible solution is offered by agencies which follow such a gender-neutral statement with information detailing further aspects of domestic violence. For example, The Children's Society's Wyrley Birch Centre (see Case Study 2, Chapter 4) worked on a definition beginning with a gender-neutral statement and then went on to say:

> 1) domestic violence is predominantly abuse of women and children by men; and 2) domestic violence causes children to suffer harm which is frequently unheard and unrecognised. (From an unpublished internal policy document)

Barnardo's provides a different emphasis in its follow-up statement:

> In the main, men are usually the perpetrators of abuse and women the victims.... However, some Barnardo's projects have seen an increase in men who have reported violence to them from their female partners. This clearly needs to be appropriately worked with and addressed, as does violence which occurs within some Lesbian and Gay relationships. (Barnardo's, 1997, p 4)

Other issues, including the ongoing nature of domestic violence, the range of behaviours and the seriousness of the impact, are then outlined.

In summary, many organisations, including some multi-agency forums, use gender-neutral statements as the starting point of their definition. However, providing further detail concerning gender and other aspects of complexity in a more lengthy statement allows a more inclusive process to occur when, for example, a range of organisations meet to work on a comprehensive domestic violence strategy.

Sub-indicator: Definitions should acknowledge the issue of power and control

An indicator of good practice emerging from the study was the recognition within the statement that the abuse of power and control by one person over another is central to domestic violence. While statements to this effect were in the minority, they were often associated with the organisations or areas where work on domestic violence was most developed or developing rapidly.

For example, Bath and North East Somerset Housing and Social Services borrows the following definition from Mullender and Humphreys (1998):

> Domestic violence typically involves a pattern of physical, sexual and emotional abuse and intimidation which escalates in frequency and severity over time. It can be understood as the misuse of power and the exercise of control by one partner over the other in an intimate relationship, usually by a man over a woman, occasionally by a woman over a man (though without the same pattern of societal collusion), and also occurring amongst same-sex couples. It has profound consequences in the lives of individuals, families and communities.

This definition succinctly recognises a number of elements which are central to domestic violence:

- the issue of power and control;
- a range of behaviours;
- escalation over time;
- the social collusion in gendered pattern of violence, with women more likely to be abused;
- diversity, including that woman may abuse men and that it occurs between same sex couples;
- the wide-ranging impact of domestic violence.

Summary

The development of an agreed definition of domestic violence is an important step for an organisation. Definitions may need to recognise that there are a range of organisations that work in the area, as well as many people who experience domestic violence. Statements which acknowledge diversity as well as the dominant gendered pattern of violence against women may allow for a greater level of inclusion and avoid potentially long and contentious debates. Domestic violence usually entails more than one assault, and may include a range of psychological, mental, sexual and financial abuses. The establishment of power and control of one person (usually a man) over another (usually a woman) is a defining feature of domestic violence.

Good Practice Indicator 2: Monitoring and screening – knowing the extent of the problem

Domestic violence screening and monitoring involves the systematic collection and regular collation of data from service users concerning whether or not they have experienced or are experiencing domestic violence. There have been research findings showing that services using domestic violence screening and monitoring are aware of a much higher level of incidence among service users than services without screening or monitoring (Hester et al, 1997; Hester and Pearson, 1998). The following sub-indicators regarding good practice in relation to screening and monitoring were identified in the survey and questionnaire data.

Sub-indicator: Systematic screening using a protocol of questions

How and when to ask about domestic violence were concerns that arose from the survey data. With regard to 'how to ask', direct questions about 'domestic violence' may not be particularly useful. Thus, some projects had devised a dedicated questionnaire or list of questions asking about the elements that make up domestic violence, that is, experiences of assault, forced sex, threat, fear, being shouted at, feeling humiliated and so on, and children might be asked about the way things are at home. As for 'when to ask', projects with well-developed screening approaches in the study were asking routinely at the initial referral stage, as part of an intake process, and/or every time a client was seen.

Screening was considered a useful way of raising awareness of domestic violence among both clients and staff as it provides an indication that domestic violence is taken seriously by the agency concerned.

> One NSPCC project was in the early stages of routinely asking women they work with directly about experiences of domestic violence, rather than merely talking about the issue indirectly, as they had done previously. The respondent commented:
>
> > "If you ask a woman about domestic violence – eg whether she has been or is currently subject to it – including sexual assault of her – it gives the message that she will be listened to, if at a later date she feels safe enough, to talk about her experiences."

> One health visitor service in Northern Ireland had established a pilot project to routinely ask mothers with new babies questions related to abuse. They ask mothers two or three questions about domestic violence at least once during the postnatal period, which are repeated at a later visit if the worker has concerns. The mothers are told that everyone is being asked a few questions about domestic violence, and are also asked whether this is okay. If so, they are asked the following:
>
> - If your partner or someone in your family were hurting you, do you have someone to talk to?
> - Do you know where you could get help if you or someone you know were being hurt by a partner?
> - Have you been hurt or threatened by a partner or family member? OR Does your partner ever make you feel afraid?

Most of the statutory sector and children's charities projects surveyed had not yet established such fully developed means of attaining information concerning domestic violence. They might only ask a simple, general question for monitoring purposes, or in relation to only part of

their work. For instance some social services teams only asked about domestic violence specifically in relation to child protection conferences. Many of the children's charity projects said that information concerning domestic violence was often attained only incidentally with regard to their work with children, and/or they waited for the issue to be mentioned.

There were also some worrying examples where it was suggested that screening would be inappropriate or not possible. One children's charity project gave as a reason for not asking about domestic violence that they were using a 'child-centred' approach and therefore only worked with information provided, without prompting the child. Another project suggested that their shift in work orientation from doing assessment to providing treatment meant that domestic violence was no longer obvious. Yet neither a 'child-centred' approach nor treatment should preclude asking the children about domestic violence; both approaches are much more effective if they incorporate such questions, as shown by the resulting positive work with children documented by another Joseph Rowntree Foundation project (Hester and Pearson, 1998).

Sub-indicator: Mechanisms for recording

Even though domestic violence monitoring data may underestimate the actual levels of domestic violence due to difficulties of disclosure, recording and collation, such data provide important information with regard to practice and service provision. We obtained a number of monitoring forms as part of the survey, and it was apparent that some of the national organisations required monitoring information concerning domestic violence to be provided by local projects. In other instances, local projects had added domestic violence to the list of items on the national form.

Sub-indicator: Guidance and supervision

Asking about domestic violence can be difficult, and staff may not see the relevance of domestic violence to their work. It is important for staff to examine these issues in supervision and for organisations to issue guidance at both local and national levels. Apart from the specialist agencies (for example, refuges and women's services) which now monitor their referrals comprehensively, the projects with some of the clearest guidance concerning screening and monitoring were the children's charity projects carrying out family mediation and affiliated to the national umbrella organisation for mediators, National Family Mediation (see Hester et al, 1997). We were provided with examples of local screening policies based on this good practice guidance, although they were less detailed and therefore more open to individual interpretation.

Sub-indicator: Training

How to ask about domestic violence and when to ask are important issues for training emerging from this study and others, and are detailed in the DoH training resource, *Making an impact* (Barnardo's et al, 1998). Training on how to operate procedures sensitively and what to do on disclosure is vital for staff conducting screening.

Sub-indicator: Feedback mechanisms

Monitoring provides a benchmark in relation to evaluation of service provision, allowing realistic and useful evaluation questions to be devised.

Summary

The use of screening indicates that a service has thought about the importance of ascertaining whether or not domestic violence is an issue for service users, has looked at ways of asking about this, and thus has developed a more safety-oriented practice (Hester et al, 1997). Use of monitoring indicates that a service has mechanisms for recording information concerning the incidence of domestic violence, and this may enable more effective support and resourcing to be put in place. However, it is also vital that adequate supervision and training for staff accompany screening processes.

Good Practice Indicator 3: Policies and guidelines – guiding the work to be done

Good practice is represented by agencies which, even where domestic violence is not central to their work, have developed a domestic violence policy to assist staff and managers. Policies and guidelines often need to be developed for two different, but inter-related contexts: the multi-agency context and the specific organisational or professional context. The development of good practice guidelines and policies locally and nationally is now a feature of domestic violence policy across the board (see, for example, the new national *Resource manual for health services* produced by the DoH: Brasse, 2000). In the present study, the quantitative data, analysis of documents attached to questionnaires and the qualitative information revealed useful data about the broad picture in relation to good practice guidelines.

While the qualitative data reveal that excellent policy documents and guidelines are now available, the statistical data (see Table 17) show that fewer than half of the social services departments which responded to the survey have policies on domestic violence in place. Similarly, in spite of the extensive work by children's charities in the area of domestic violence and the development of quite comprehensive practice guidance nationally, it was surprising to find that only a minority of local projects appeared to draw on such national policy to develop their project policies. Conversley, even though Women's Aid groups are autonomous organisations within their own national federations, wide-ranging support networks and codes of guidance exist to facilitate coordination and refuge and outreach services usually do work to specific principles and good practice guidelines.

Table 17: Specific domestic violence guidelines

DV guidelines	Yes		No		Being developed		Total	
	Number	%	Number	%	Number	%	Number	%
Social services departments and trusts (Northern Ireland)	45	39.4	52	45.6	17	15	114	100
Children's charities	70	15.6	379	84.4	0	0	449	100
Women's Aid	326	100	0	0	0	0	326	100

In the study, we identified a range of sub-indicators of good practice in relation to policy and practice guidance.

Sub-indicator: Safety and confidentiality

Clearly, the development of policies and guidelines on domestic violence is not necessarily an indicator of good practice as some policies are better than others. While most policies refer to safety and confidentiality for survivors of domestic violence as a central tenet, good practice is indicated by policies that give specific guidance on these issues. For example, Cheshire County Council (1998) and Gloucestershire Social Services (1999) stress the need to inform women clearly about the boundaries of confidentiality and explore how they might be safely contacted.

These guidelines contrast with areas where there is an unhelpful, undifferentiated flow of information (referral) from the police to social services following any incident of domestic violence where children are involved, or where letters are sent from either the police or social services highlighting to both parents the fact that domestic violence has destructive effects on children witnessing this behaviour. Such procedures can lead to coordinated and standardised responses, but may sometimes occur without the woman's consent or knowledge and may lead to a sense of increased monitoring and surveillance, but not necessarily of increased service provision.

In many cases, however, onward referral is targeted. Some police services operate a graded system in which social services are contacted only in specific circumstances: for example, after a certain number of call-outs (for example, two or three) or according to the severity of the assault or the overall situation. Birmingham Social Services and Birmingham Police (and several other localities, including Solihull and Hertfordshire) operate a protocol which specifically flags up children on the child protection register for an inter-agency response (although this system is likely to exclude many other children in need).

Guidelines which list a range of 'dos' and 'don'ts' for frontline practitioners, prioritising the safety of women and children, can be considered helpful (see, for example, London Borough of Hammersmith and Fulham, 1995). NCH Action

for Children provides a comprehensive list of practice implications to guide workers in the following areas: child protection issues; contact with fathers; responses to violent men; responses to women who are experiencing domestic violence and responses to children (NCH Action for Children, 1997).

Sub-indicator: Involvement of the survivors of domestic violence and their representatives in refuge and advocacy services

Mistakes about safe policies would be less likely to occur if primary users of the services were consulted. The Fife Multi-Agency Domestic Violence Forum (1996, 1999) began with a consultation with women who had experienced domestic violence, asking them particularly about their experiences of seeking help. The Forum's strategy has developed from this base, alongside participation and consultation with young people. Other areas, such as Bedfordshire, have written into their social and community care plan that:

> Children who have experienced domestic violence should be consulted and have a voice in the services they need. This would provide an opportunity to include children's experiences of domestic violence when planning children's services. (Bedfordshire County Council, 1999, Point 5.2)

Now that much policy development is occurring as part of a corporate, or wider multi-agency strategy for an area, it is particularly challenging to create thoughtful processes that encourage participation from abused women and their children, which result in a meaningful contribution of their views and needs for progressing future practice, and which avoid tokenism or compromising safety.

Good practice in the study was indicated by strategies that ensured the refuge movement and other women's support and advocacy projects retained a central role in consulting with survivors and in the development of policy and practice guidance. However, the survey indicated that, despite a wide range of initiatives put in place by, or in partnership with, Women's Aid and other independent women's services, these services were often underfunded and many were somewhat marginalised within wider strategy and policy formulation.

Sub-indicator: Attention to diversity and equality

In some localities, attention to diversity and equality within the policies used stands out, and is a clear indicator of good practice (for example, London Borough of Newham, 1994-97; Doncaster Metropolitan Borough Council, 1997; Cheshire County Council, 1998; London Borough of Hammersmith and Fulham, 1998; Leeds City Council Department of Social Services, undated, to mention just a few). Indications of good practice were shown by:

- a clear and unequivocal general statement about equality and diversity at the beginning of a policy;
- a detailed statement within the policy about the particular needs and access issues for black women, disabled women and other groups who may face specific barriers to gaining help;
- user involvement and reviewing strategies;
- specific service provision;
- training which embeds the policy in a context which makes a difference to the lives of women and children affected.

Doncaster Domestic Violence Working Party has developed a comprehensive section in their manual on the 'Issues affecting particular women'. These include sections on Black women; issues of class; younger women; women with disabilities; older women; lesbians; gypsy/traveller women and women working in prostitution (Doncaster Metropolitan Borough Council, 1997).

The projects in the children's charities frequently had detailed policies on equalities, including gender equality policies (nearly three quarters of the sample) although not specifically written in relation to domestic violence practice.

Sub-indicator: Working together within a wider strategy

Surprisingly, a significant number of social services departments (70%) appeared to be developing guidelines independently of any wider domestic violence strategy for the locality in question. While 'one-off' guidelines of this type within a department have value, an indicator of best practice is the development of policies as part of a wider strategy, both within the organisation and the broad multi-agency setting.

City of Bradford Metropolitan Council Policy

Bradford has produced policy and good practice guidelines which include a general statement of council policy; general information on domestic violence; good practice guidelines for all workers; good practice guidelines for specific areas of work; and information on services and resources for women fleeing domestic violence. A manual has also been produced which provides guidance on the development of policy and guidelines in the area of domestic violence (a useful tool for the large group of local authorities which have not yet produced these) (City of Bradford, undated).

The London Borough of Hammersmith and Fulham is currently re-working its policies and guidelines to reflect the new initiative in the area – Standing Together – which is developing a full inter-agency response to domestic violence based on the Duluth Model. Gloucestershire Social Services (1999) is similarly developing a comprehensive inter-agency strategy with a referral and tracking system. The Leeds Inter-agency Project (Leeds City Council Department of Social Services, undated), the London Borough of Newham (1994-97), the three-year London Borough of Islington project – Domestic Violence Matters (Kelly, 1999), and the Croydon One Stop Project (London Borough of Croydon, 1999) provide examples of particularly strong inter-agency strategies which incorporate both the voluntary and statutory sectors in the development of policies and guidelines. Fife Multi-Agency Domestic Violence Forum (1999) developed an innovative inter-agency conference (the Jigsaw Conference) to highlight the gaps and create action plans for both policy and service initiatives.

Sub-indicator: Development of a broad range of policies, guidelines and clarity in the referral system

While not all areas are developing such systematic and comprehensive responses to domestic violence, it is clear that effective work in this area requires a broad range of policies. Pryke and Thomas (1998) have suggested that local authorities need policies to cover the following areas:

- children and families (including drawing up guidelines which differentiate policies for children in need, and policies for child protection);
- vulnerable adults (which may be incorporated into a wider policy statement on community care);
- violent men or perpetrators (including policies for staff safety procedures, and policies and guidelines for investigation, assessment and programmes of work with perpetrators);
- providing information for service users (including services available, eligibility for services, relevant powers and duties of a department, service user responsibilities and complaints procedures);
- practice guidelines for frontline workers.

We would add domestic violence policy development in housing, education, youthwork, policing and community development and inter-agency coordination. Good practice is indicated by areas and organisations which have given attention to the broad scope of policy development.

Sub-indicator: Building on policies which have already been well developed in other areas

A criticism sometimes levelled at inter-agency forums is that they are 'talking shops' where lengthy discussion about policy has taken precedence over the development of increased provision for survivors or perpetrators of violence. Given that some areas have a 10-year history of work in this area, there is no reason for each locality to be developing policy from scratch. These policies then need to be developed, 'owned' and adapted to suit the particular organisational or inter-agency context. A good example is provided in Fife where the housing officer for the homelessness unit researched housing policies on domestic violence in the UK, and then built on these to develop the Fife domestic violence housing policy, including a good practice tenancy agreement. A significant amount of inter-agency policy development around the country has been based on work initially undertaken by the London Boroughs of Islington (1995) and Hammersmith and Fulham (1995).

Sub-indicator: Policies embedded within the organisation

Policies remain empty rhetoric unless appropriate training and supervision are provided to integrate the policy into agency practice. Some organisations showed uneven development in this area with a well-written policy but no parallel training.

Gloucestershire Social Services (1999) *Department policy on domestic violence* provides a comprehensive approach to policy development. As part of the policy, all teams are to be provided with an information and resource file to enable staff to develop good practice. Targets on staff training, reorganising the information and referral system, and reviewing the policy are all identified.

Policies often require the development of services. For example, some areas have appropriately written policies that draw distinctions between different thresholds of referral for assessment and investigation to either the family support team or child protection team. However, in some of these same areas, the service provision for women and children in situations of domestic violence is minimal, raising the question of how the policy on family support could possibly be implemented.

Sub-indicator: Detailed guidelines

Improved practice is often defeated by managers' lack of detailed thinking about the barriers that have created insensitive work in this area. While the problem is sometimes that too much procedural detail can constrain professional discretion, it was clear from an analysis of policies and guidelines in our samples, that detail was often an indication of a well-thought through policy to tackle the change in direction required and the barriers to making that shift.

Warwickshire Social Services Department (1999), *Domestic violence guidance for social work staff*, provides detailed guidelines for workers in children's services on referral action (including how retrospective recording of information about domestic violence will occur); issues for assessment; immediate safety issues; working with the child protection procedures (including guidance on child protection conferences); staff care and safety.

National Family Mediation (NFM) policy

The NFM policy begins with a statement about the relevance of a domestic violence policy and sets the context for the policy in good practice principles in relation to family mediation. A detailed statement highlights seven points on the implications and the process of screening and focuses on the means through which good practice will then be developed in this area (NFM, 1998).

Summary

An analysis of the questionnaires, attached documents and case study information gathered in this study suggested that the development of domestic violence policy has been uneven. Good practice indicators include policies and guidelines which demonstrate the following:

- attention to safety and confidentiality for survivors of domestic violence;
- involvement of service users and their direct representatives in the development of policies;
- attention to the issues of diversity and equality;
- working together in a wider inter-agency strategy;
- recognising the centrality of women's refuge, support and advocacy services within this;
- a broad range of policies and guidelines;
- efficient use of policy developments undertaken in other areas;
- embedding policies in the organisation through training and service development;
- detailed guidelines particularly in areas where a change of practice is required.

Good Practice Indicator 4: Safety measures and safety-oriented practice

Safety is a crucial issue in any circumstance where domestic violence may be an issue. Four sub-indicators concerning safety were identified in the mapping survey.

Sub-indicator: Safety planning

Safety planning is a key practical strategy which aims to help individual women and children stay safe. It involves separate planning with women and children in a practical and detailed way, including:

- asking women and children to identify a safe place to go if there is further violence;
- asking women and children to identify a person they can go to if necessary;
- ensuring that women and children know how to contact emergency services safely;
- making sure children understand that it is neither safe nor their responsibility to intervene to try and protect their mothers;
- undertaking very detailed work with women about locks, access to the telephone, and so on.

Imani, a support group in south west London associated with NCH Action for Children, makes detailed safety plans with, and offers very practical safety advice to, abused women and children. They also offer concrete 'back-up' assistance, such as safekeeping of women's passports and immigration documents.

Barnardo's Domestic Violence Outreach Scheme in Northern Ireland carries out safety planning with both women and children. Women's safety is monitored with them every time they attend the project, and they have their own detailed safety plans in place. When a member of the research team met two children who had been helped by the scheme a year later, both could remember their safety plans (for example, a safe place to go, a trusted person to talk to, safe ways of summoning help, taking care of a younger sibling during a violent incident) and both were still able to use them if needed.

While all of the Women's Aid projects and most of the perpetrators' programmes provided women with help regarding safety planning, the statutory sector and children's charities (despite the two exceptional examples above) did not appear to use this approach to any noticeable extent and there is clearly a need for them to develop safety planning in relation to both children and women.

Sub-indicator: A range of organisational measures

At an organisational level it is important to have safety measures in place for premises, attendance, confidentiality, provision of information and links with other agencies.

All the work of Women's Aid is focused on ensuring the safety of women and children, and this is reflected in the provision of safe accommodation as well as their other activities, including advice lines and outreach services.

> The Hereford refuge was purpose built, with a 'smart' entry phone incorporating a video camera and a separate 999 telephone. Rules on safety are clear and firmly enforced. They are also rephrased carefully for children in ways which can be easily understood.

Perpetrators' projects highlight the importance of having a differential approach to confidentiality to ensure safety for partners, whereby men's rights to confidentiality are limited while any input from partners is kept confidential from perpetrators. Perpetrators' projects also talked of keeping the supervising probation officer of mandated men abreast of any safety concerns, and informing police and social services of any disclosure of child abuse.

> With regard to men and safety planning, one children's charity-run project explained that: "The men sign an agreement making it clear that there will be active liaison with the police if we have any doubts about the safety of children or women".

However, there were worrying gaps in safety policy in some projects including lack of child protection policies, omitting the perspective of women's organisations in the design and delivery of their programmes, and not involving partners for feedback or not notifying them if men failed to attend or were asked to leave a programme.

The statutory sector and children's charities tended to be ad hoc in their approaches to wider safety, using a range of measures as and when they saw these as appropriate. The children's charities provided numerous examples, including the use of child protection measures, ensuring the child was safe before work commenced, and gathering information about who could collect the child from the project. Measures for women's safety might involve use of separate rooms and/or having two workers present in mediation sessions, and abusers not being informed if their partners were also on the premises.

Sub-indicator: Supporting mothers as a response to child protection

It was clear from respondents that an increasing number of agencies were adopting the approach of supporting the safety of non-abusive mothers as a positive response in child protection where domestic violence is an issue. This is also the practice orientation suggested in DoH guidance as outlined in Chapter 1, and corresponds with a 'children's needs' approach (see Hester et al, 1998/2000, Chapter 8).

> **Barnardo's Domestic Violence Outreach Scheme in Northern Ireland**
>
> One woman from this scheme commented, "They realise here that you're not going to help the kids as a family unless you help the mum, and if you help the mum you're helping the kids".

Sub-indicator: Worker's safety

Protecting workers from perpetrators of violence was identified as important by respondents, and a much larger proportion of the children's charities projects had safety measures in place for workers than for women and children. Such measures included use of mobile phones, working in pairs, recording whereabouts and applying risk assessment procedures.

Summary

The mapping survey and case studies provided evidence of a wide range of safety measures being used by projects, as well as the use of safety planning with individuals. However, the use of safety measures was ad hoc in many projects, they were not always applied consistently and there was often a lack of attention to safety planning. Some projects also appeared to have paid greater attention to workers' safety than to the safety of service users. These are clearly areas for improvement.

Good Practice Indicator 5: Training – raising awareness, exploring values, developing skills

A key component for ensuring the effectiveness of domestic violence intervention lies in the development of training. As a result, domestic violence training has developed in recent years, both within individual agencies and on a multi-agency basis.

From the survey, it could be seen that practice in this area, as in all others, was extremely varied. The general results from the questionnaires are shown in Table 18.

While the figures broadly show whether any training has been delivered in an area, care needs to be taken not to read too much into these statistics. Since a locality which has delivered half or one day of inter-agency training still shows as a positive response. Worse, almost one third of local authority areas in this sample do not have even the most minimal awareness-raising training on domestic violence either within an organisation or on an inter-agency basis. The figures for the children's charities are of particular concern when such a large number of projects work with domestic violence issues: one quarter of the domestic violence training cited for the children's charities lasted one day or less.

A number of sub-indicators for good practice can be drawn out from an analysis of the survey and the case studies.

Sub-indicator: Training large numbers of employees

Training large numbers of employees provides a particular challenge, but one which recognises that most workers within an agency will be in contact with significant numbers of domestic violence survivors or perpetrators. Several areas or organisations have taken significant steps to mainstream training across the sector. Cheshire Inter-agency Forum, for example, provided six pilot courses, attended by 370 participants, with a follow-up specialist course on domestic violence and the law attended by 90 participants.

Lincolnshire Social Services

In Lincolnshire, the multi-agency training strategy aims to provide training places for 1,800 staff across the local authority between 1998 and 2000. The ACPC has made a commitment to train all members of staff. Training is given via initial awareness raising (a one-day course scheduled for 10 different dates), as well as in separate, specialist training on assessment, the law, seminars to launch the domestic violence campaign, and training for 150 receptionist staff (a half-day session scheduled for three different dates). The training strategy is part of a wider programme to tackle domestic violence, including a publicity campaign.

Table 18: Initial training

Initial training	Yes		No		Total	
	Number	**%**	**Number**	**%**	**Number**	**%**
Local authority	78	68.5	36	31.5	114	100
Children's charities	216	48	233	52	449	100
Women's Aid	326	100	0	0	326	100
Perpetrators programmes	25	96	1	4	26	100

Welsh, English, Scottish and Northern Ireland Women's Aids

WAFE runs a national training unit, *Women's Aid Training*, which offers wide-ranging programmes on a national and local basis. Two examples from 1998 are the provision of courses to all playworkers in Lewisham, and the comprehensive training on the 1996 Family Law Act provided for Leicester City Council (which has an officer responsible for domestic violence issues in every department).

Welsh Women's Aid coordinates training for police services throughout Wales, and also offers training services nationally and regionally to probation, social services, health services, schools and the Crown Prosecution Service. Northern Ireland Women's Aid similarly coordinates training and has produced various training guides, including *No fear, heading for healthy relationships: An activity pack for working with young people* (NIWA, 1998a) for use by youth and social workers, and *Violence on the edge: Providing effective support for minority ethnic women at risk of domestic violence in Northern Ireland* (NIWA, 1998b). Scottish Women's Aid also offers national training to various agencies (for example to the Scottish Federation of Housing Associations), particularly through multi-agency forums, and has input into various social work training courses.

Sub-indicator: Training beyond initial awareness-raising leading to a range of specialist courses

Ongoing training was a feature of local authority areas with a developed training strategy and specialist courses were frequently provided across agencies. For example, some areas provided courses on the law and domestic violence, assessment, direct work with domestic violence survivors, specific issues for black women, disabled women and lesbians in relation to domestic violence, and workshops on violence against workers.

Other areas have taken seriously the training of particular professional groups. In Northern Ireland, for instance, the Royal Group of Hospitals and Dental Hospital Health and Social Services Trust has a comprehensive training programme which is specifically tailored to the needs of accident and emergency staff, and run within that section of the hospital.

The particular issues for child protection workers were highlighted by several authorities and were usually managed through two-day training courses. Brighton and Hove has taken such training a step further by developing a programme of two-hour sessions based in children's services teams, as well as two-day courses on domestic violence and child protection. Such an approach has potential for overcoming the unevenness of training across a sector. Other areas have responded to the needs of school teaching staff in terms of domestic violence training (for example, West Sussex, and Newry and Mourne).

West Sussex

West Sussex has undertaken a planned approach to raising the issue of domestic violence with teachers. An initial questionnaire to all schools in the area led to requests for training from 18 schools. Training is now being provided through one-and-a-half-hour training sessions. A training pack has also been developed which has been further used for training church groups and magistrates.

Sub-indicator: A rolling programme of domestic violence training

A rolling programme is an indicator of a well-developed training strategy. The Scottish research (Henderson, 1997) comments that only Women's Aid workers, and to a lesser extent the police, have an ongoing programme of training on domestic violence. Other organisations and departments in Scotland have generally performed poorly on this indicator, and even the police training was very uneven. Similarly, the questionnaires from the rest of the UK showed that only a few areas had taken up the challenge to develop an ongoing programme of domestic violence training and, therefore, lacked a strategy which accounted for the fact that workers change, or may miss out on the first round of training offered. Within the children's charities, 12% provided regular up-dating of training.

Sub-indicator: The integration of the training strategy into operational planning for domestic violence services

Such integration within a locality emerged as a strength in this study. Some local authority areas, for example, have used a conference on domestic violence and child abuse to 'kick start', not only a training initiative, but a wider campaign to raise the awareness of domestic violence, sometimes through their ACPCs, and to prompt coordinated services.

Other indicators of integration were provided by areas that showed strong development across provision, training, and policy and practice guidelines (for example, Leeds Inter-agency Project, Hammersmith and Fulham). In contrast, questions about effectiveness need to be raised in areas that showed uneven progress, for example where policy and guidelines were well developed, but no training strategy for embedding the policies within the organisation or inter-agency context had been initiated.

Sub-indicator: A strategy for financing and providing ongoing training

The development of a strategy for financing and providing training is clearly a priority if work in the area is to continue. A range of different models for providing training were developing, including:

- the appointment of full-time or part-time trainers (Metropolitan Borough of Wirral, Sunderland City Council);
- the commissioning of a trainer from the Women's Aid refuge to undertake training for the inter-agency forum and social services department (Brighton and Hove; Fife Council);
- the development of training partnerships such as those between the ACPC and a seconded domestic violence worker (West Sussex);
- training provided by social services training section (Derby City Council);
- coordinated 'training the trainers' initiatives across agencies (for example Leeds Inter-agency Project).

Other areas, such as Cheshire County Council, had developed innovative ways of funding initial training, in this case, pooling £250 each from the police, probation, the health authority, education, community development and social services.

Sub-indicator: Training quality, equality issues and service users' voices

An important good practice indicator concerns the overall content of training. A good training curriculum would include attention to equality issues, the involvement at some level of women and their children who have experienced domestic violence, and the inclusion of definitions and understandings of domestic violence as developed elsewhere in this report.

Who provides the training?

Who provides domestic violence training is a contentious issue; one which is emerging as the area expands. In the past, it was predominantly Women's Aid workers who were invited to provide training as their contact with women and children in situations of domestic violence, combined with the fact that they are one of the few agencies to consistently provide training to their own workers, gives them an acknowledged expertise in the field. In many areas, Women's Aid continues to provide training services. However, as demand for training in this field escalates, and specialist needs (such as mental health assessments) are identified, many more trainers with a range of different backgrounds are emerging, with greater or lesser qualification in the area. Henderson (1997), for example, rather acerbically notes the sparse training within Scottish social work departments, which had nevertheless not prevented half of them from providing training to other organisations (Henderson, 1997, p 62).

This raises a note of warning in the training area. While this study did not explore the details of the training provided, clearly the issue of quality is an important one. The training pack commissioned by the DoH – *Making an impact: Children and domestic violence* (Barnardo's et al, 1998) – marks an attempt to increase the accessibility of good quality domestic violence training. However, the expertise of specialist workers providing frontline services to women and children should continue to be acknowledged as an important part of training provision within this expanding area.

Summary

Training to increase sensitivity, skills and the effectiveness of intervention with both survivors and perpetrators of domestic violence needs to become an essential element in transforming organisational cultures. Good practice demands a well-developed strategy, integrated across organisations – including the inter-agency initiative where there is one – and recognising the role of refuges, women's support and advocacy services in this strategy.

Good Practice Indicator 6: Evaluation – ensuring effective responses

Different considerations apply to evaluating work with survivors on the one hand (be they women, children or family groups), and work with perpetrators on the other. While evaluation in all fields is commonly accepted as constituting part of good practice, and this is no less true of family support work with women and children, there are additional reasons why evaluation is of central importance in men's work. If perpetrators' programmes are less than effective, and particularly if partners or ex-partners are given false hope about the likelihood that men will change as a result of participating in such a programme, real threats to the safety of women and children may result. Evaluation can help to guard against this, although it remains a very inexact science.

Survivors

In the children's charities, about a quarter of projects with domestic violence relevance (n = 120, 26.7%) had been evaluated. Where this had taken place as part of a wider evaluation of the agency's work or through an independent evaluator, domestic violence expertise had not always been applied to the measurement of success or effectiveness. Within the statutory sector, mainstream services are often subject to routine monitoring, although questions of effectiveness in response to domestic violence are not typically the subject of evaluation. The research study indicated a lack of evaluation of Women's Aid services, although new projects were more likely to have built in costsings to allow evaluation to occur.

Perpetrators programmes

Of 18 responses to the relevant section of the survey of perpetrators' programmes, all but three mentioned current or recent evaluations, although, again, not all of these were conducted by evaluators who had particular domestic violence expertise. Despite these efforts, there were some notable shortcomings, including in respect of the measures used and the timescale involved (see below). In addition, it was two, three or even four years since some programmes had been evaluated so current data were not available. Also, given the low completion rates reported by most groups, rates of change would tend to relate only to a low proportion of those referred. Overall, it is not possible to say with any certainty whether these programmes were successful in their stated aim of ending men's violence; this is currently a matter of national concern to the Home Office, which is funding a national evaluation of two 'Pathfinder Programmes' in this field.

Sub-indicators of good practice for evaluation in the field of domestic violence have been identified as the following.

Sub-indicator: Independent evaluation

Evaluations conducted by practitioners themselves on their own work, while valuable, typically carry less weight than those conducted independently by someone external to the project. For example, half the perpetrators' programmes surveyed had recognised this and had called on independent, external evaluators.

In a complex field such as this, however, it was clear from the issues highlighted in the mapping study that a simple knowledge of evaluative techniques is not sufficient; it is vital that evaluations are based on an adequate knowledge of domestic violence. With perpetrators' groups in particular, it is important to know the international literature (see summary in Mullender and Burton, 2000) and to understand the key role of partner reports and of follow-up (see below).

Sub-indicator: Building in the voice of survivors

In respect of work with women and/or children, it is important that survivors' own views are sought about the services they have received. This includes asking whether they have been helped to feel safe, as well as whether they consider other service aims to have been met.

For perpetrators' programmes, it remains the survivors' rather than the perpetrators' voices which are the most essential to hear. Self-report by perpetrators (together with all forms of official records) is liable to extreme under-reporting of further abuse. Partner report has been shown to be the most valid and reliable measure of success (Gondolf, 1998b), and any programme which wants to demonstrate effectiveness needs to take seriously the views of partners (including ex-partners and new partners). Partners should be asked about any repeat violence and also about their quality of life if they continue to live with, or to be in touch with, the perpetrator after he completes the group. This is to ensure that he has not substituted emotional abuse, or other tactics of power and control, for physical abuse. Three of the perpetrator programmes surveyed had had evaluations which did not include partner report. This would make them of questionable value.

Sub-indicator: Follow-up

Wherever possible in work with survivors, it is helpful to ensure that women and children remain safe some time after they initially sought emergency help. This is important because patterns of abuse can escalate when it becomes clear that the woman is contemplating seeking outside help or separating from her partner, and after she actually does so. Follow-up overlaps with continued screening; the Barnardo's Domestic Violence Outreach Scheme (DVOS), Northern Ireland, asks women on each occasion they visit the project whether they have been safe in the intervening period.

In perpetrators' programmes, it is essential that follow-up information is sought, at least six and preferably 12 months after the group has ended, since any changes that are noted in men participating may not be maintained (see Mullender and Burton, 2000, for a summary of the literature on this). In the survey, two programmes did refer to a longer-term follow-up, one after six months and the other after one year.

Sub-indicator: Feedback loop

The purpose of evaluation is not only to measure outcomes ('what works'), but also to identify areas of practice in which change is needed. In both respects, it is important to feed back from evaluation into policy and practice. The perpetrators' programmes surveyed, for instance, were able to give several examples of improvements made after evaluation had taken place. These included introducing contact with partners, including content on children and on sexual abuse in the group, lengthening the programme, and restructuring content to include more behavioural work. In work with women and children, the Wyrley Birch Centre is an example of a project which has evaluated process as well as content, building its emphasis on being both child- and woman-centred.

Summary

No innovative project can 'spread the word' with confidence about its work unless that work has been properly and independently evaluated. There are some particular considerations in respect of domestic violence which mean that evaluators require domestic violence expertise. The evaluation of work with domestic violence perpetrators is particularly challenging, with a major international literature pointing out both the complexities and some of the ways forward, notably seeking the views of partners and ensuring adequate follow-up. The messages from evaluation need to feed back into practice so that it continues to develop and improve.

Good Practice Indicator 7: Multi-agency coordination – working together

The multi-agency approach is currently promoted widely, although often in a rather unspecific way, as a policy and practice option in domestic violence work, and as a desirable outcome. While we did not specifically survey inter-agency responses in this study, the data collected, supplemented by other studies (such as Hague et al, 1996b), offers some insight into these claims. Numerous partnerships and inter-agency projects were identified during the research, as noted throughout this report.

A good practice indicator to emerge from this and other studies is, indeed, multi-agency coordination. However, by this we do not mean solely establishing inter-agency domestic violence forums. Rather we refer to the coordination, or even, in some cases, integration of service provision and policy development so that agencies work to the same brief and adopt a consistent approach. The setting up of inter-agency forums is a tool with which to work towards this 'end', rather than being the 'end' in itself.

There is clearly value in multi-agency forums as demonstrated by the wide variety of domestic violence responses described in the survey questionnaires in which the work of such a forum had played a part. We did not, in this short study, collect information about the functioning, organisation or structure of these multi-agency forums or their work programmes. However, the 1996 Hague, Malos and Dear study (Hague et al, 1996b) lists their work as including:

- monitoring domestic violence services, identifying gaps in service and attempting to fill these gaps;
- coordinating service provision;
- improving practice by developing domestic violence strategies, policies and practice guidelines, and initiating domestic violence training;
- engaging in preventative, educational and awareness-raising work (including developing perpetrators' programmes, public education campaigns, education packs for schools etc) (Hague et al, 1996b; Hague and Malos, 1996).

In conducting this work, inter-agency domestic violence forums form one part of a wider effort to coordinate provision, together with specific, one-off multi-agency partnerships to achieve specific

Fife Multi-agency Domestic Violence Forum

The Fife Multi-agency Domestic Violence Forum has been meeting since 1993. Its aims have been underpinned by a commitment to:

- adequate provision of support services for women and children;
- appropriate legal protection for women and children suffering from violence;
- active prevention of crimes of violence against women and children.

Of particular note in the Fife Domestic Violence Strategy have been the attention to the experiences of women and young people, and a strong preventative focus based in strategies of community participation through the three-year zero-tolerance campaign.

The Fife Multi-agency Domestic Violence Forum underpinned its strategy with a consultation about service provision that included focus groups and interviews with women who had contact with Women's Aid refuges and outreach services. Their experiences of seeking help were used to assist in identifying gaps in service provision. Consultation with young people occurred through sustained and innovative project work in schools and youth groups, the organisation and running of a young people's conference – 'Voices of the Future' – and high involvement of young people in Fife in a research project by the Zero Tolerance Charitable Trust (1998) – *Young people's attitudes toward violence, sex and relationships*. Women's Aid has been recognised as a core service in representing the voices and experiences of women and children in situations of domestic violence. This is shown through:

- the provision of a long-term service agreement by Fife Council which secures the funding for Women's Aid;
- a shift to Women's Aid chairing the inter-agency forum;
- increased resources to Women's Aid in recognition that the Zero Tolerance strategy would increase demand on services;
- resourcing their outreach service as an integral part of service delivery through the provision of a house in which the office, the youth group and women's groups can be run;
- involvement of Women's Aid workers in training and consultation (Fife Multi-agency Domestic Violence Forum, 1996, 1999).

tasks (such as between refuges, children's charities and ACPCs) (see Home Office, 2000b).

A great deal of energy has been put into inter-agency initiatives and forums in recent years leading to some improvements in policy, particularly by the statutory sector. However, consultation for the study confirmed that it is important for multi-agency responses to avoid the 'talking shop' or 'smokescreen' outcome identified in previous studies (Hague et al, 1996b). In this scenario, agencies meet together to network and to attempt to coordinate services, but, in reality, little changes and the safety of women and children experiencing domestic violence is not improved in any perceivable way. Although networking is useful, inter-agency work should lead to changes and improvements in practice, in the medium term at least. If it fails to do so, it could perhaps be abandoned – there is nothing magic or prescriptive about this approach.

Sub-indicators of good practice within this broad attempt to coordinate services are similar to those discussed in the section on policies and strategies and are only discussed briefly here.

Sub-indicator: Consistency of service across and within agencies

Consistency across and between agencies is a vital indicator of best practice, so that an integrated approach is achieved, rather than the fragmented or inconsistent one that is present in many areas. This also entails the recognition of domestic violence as a key issue within the structural and organisational priorities of relevant agencies.

Sub-indicator: Confidentiality, permission and agreement

Attention to issues of confidentiality and permission is of importance within multi-agency coordination, as well as within other aspects of domestic violence work. It is important that women and children who have experienced domestic violence give their agreement to inter-agency liaison on individual cases, where this occurs; that civil rights are protected; and that disempowering, procedural collaboration (in which the voices of those actually involved are marginalised) is avoided.

Sub-indicator: The full and active involvement of women's refuge, outreach and support services

Within the qualitative data collected from Women's Aid, some difficulties were highlighted in the role of women's refuges and advocacy services within multi-agency initiatives in terms of their possible marginalisation. Concrete policies need to be in place to preserve the central and key position of these services as domestic violence continues to become an issue of mainstream concern to other agencies. Attempts also need to be made through forums and multi-agency collaboration to facilitate capacity building and funding for the refuge movement and the diverse services which it provides.

Sub-indicator: Equality issues and active consultation with abused women and children

Similarly, some concern was evident about the potential for overlooking equality issues and the voices and views of women and children who have experienced domestic violence, as multi-agency work moves towards being a mainstream response. Thus, attention to equality issues and to effective mechanisms for consulting with and responding to the expressed views of service users about policy development and coordinated service provision are important factors within inter-agency coordination (Hague et al, forthcoming). Concrete consultative and participative mechanisms clearly need to be put in place to enable provision to be informed by survivors views (as discussed in previous sections) and by action on equalities.

Sub-indicator: Clarity of response

Clarity of response is essential to avoid multi-agency 'fudging' in which actions, responsibilities and outcomes are unclear. Thus, mechanisms are needed to ensure clarity about decisions made, actions to be taken, lines of accountability, financial responsibilities and so on, where many organisations with different briefs and responsibilities are attempting to work together.

Sub-indicator: Monitoring of effectiveness and evaluation of inter-agency coordination

Monitoring and evaluation of multi-agency work is currently unusual but, as for single-agency responses, is important for judging effectiveness in terms of service users' views, improved provision, consistency of response, and enhanced safety for abused women and children.

Sub-indicator: Improved resourcing

An essential factor is adequate resourcing by central and local government and by other agencies to facilitate both multi-agency collaboration and service provision and development. Without improved resourcing, other practice indicators stand little chance of being achievable.

Summary

While not surveying inter-agency forums specifically, this mapping study has demonstrated that there are many innovative multi-agency attempts currently to improve services for, and practice with, families where there is domestic violence. However, the final sub-indicator above should act as a clarion call that, unless resources are provided in a coordinated fashion to meet the needs of such families (with the refuge movement and its many services remaining centre stage, alongside social, housing and health services, children's organisations, and the police and criminal justice system), progress on responses to domestic violence will inevitably be limited.

Good Practice Indicator 8: Guidelines for practical working with women and children

The previous seven indicators relate to both strategic and operational issues within agencies; however, all practice interventions (including perpetrators' programmes) need to include a practical focus on the needs of women and children experiencing domestic violence. There are clear good practice standards to be applied in how work with abused women and children is actually conducted. A list of sub-indicators was derived mainly from the qualitative evidence of the mapping study, from related consultations and from the evidence of previous research (see for example, Hester et al, 1998/2000). This was used to form the basis for practical criteria developed to select and conduct our case studies (the findings from which further illustrated and refined the list).

Directly derived from the study, this non-exhaustive list of indicators for good practice with abused women and children (most of which are referred to throughout this report) includes:

- Attention to **the voices and expressed needs of women using the service** (and their active involvement where possible).
- Attention to **children's needs and views** and recognition that these may overlap with, but not necessarily be the same as those of their mothers.
- The **empowerment of abused women and children**.
- Attention to **equalities issues and anti-discriminatory practice**.
- Attempts to **mainstream the service** within multi-agency provision.
- **Monitoring** and **evaluation**.

In general, the study confirmed other research and practice evidence (Hester et al, 1998/2000) that supporting mothers is an effective means of supporting and protecting children, even though women's and children's experiences are different and may require separate, but linked, provision. The separation of women's and children's needs is particularly important if children have also been subjected to abuse by their mothers. Assessment will need to recognise and consider the extent to which a violence-free environment contributes to the emergence of a different parenting style once the mother is no longer managing her own abuse.

These general good practice indicators all relate to the following principles of practical intervention (derived from this and other studies; see, for example, Taylor-Browne, 2000) which underlie and run through all aspects of work with abused women and children:

- Underlying all provision and service development, **the first and main priority must be improvements in safety for women and children experiencing abuse** (and including detailed safety plans).
- **The adoption of a believing, sensitive approach** to abused women and their children.
- **The provision of resourced, effective services** in both the statutory and voluntary sectors, promptly and non-judgmentally (including housing, legal, criminal justice, health and social services, one-to-one work, advocacy, refuge provision and outreach).

- **The development of specific and diverse services** in relation to minority ethnic and other communities and to women and children from diverse backgrounds (for example, for disabled women and children).

In the qualitative work and case studies, these various dimensions of good practice in work with women and children experiencing domestic violence were considered within a variety of settings and types of provision, including family support provision, community development, confidential separate provision for women and children where required, and specific provision in relation to the needs of all minority communities, including those of ethnic minority women and children.

A framework summarising the above good practice indicators is offered in the conclusion to this report.

4

Case studies

The seven case studies that follow illustrate innovative practice in a range of settings. Each project shows some, although not all, of the good practice indicators and most have yet to be evaluated.

Case Study 1: Imani: This project is supported by NCH Action for Children. It is an example of a community development and women's empowerment project in an urban milieu, developing good practice with women and children from minority ethnic communities.

Case Study 2: Wyrley Birch Centre for Parents and Children: This project is operated by The Children's Society, and provides an example of a family support project in which particular attention is paid to children's needs and voices.

Case Study 3: Domestic Violence Outreach Scheme, Northern Ireland: This is a Barnardo's project in Northern Ireland and demonstrates a particular emphasis on safety planning, children's work and women's groups.

Case Study 4: Hayle Family Support Project: This centres on a joint project between the NSPCC and the local refuge, and is included as an example of a rural project offering a family support setting.

Case Study 5: Hereford Women's Aid: This is a Women's Aid refuge and outreach project, included as an example of a provider of safe, confidential accommodation and services, and a key player in local multi-agency coordination.

Case Studies 6 and 7: Fife and the London Borough of Newham: Both Fife and Newham are included as examples of statutory authorities where large amounts of local inter-agency work are occurring, and which feature, in varying ways, innovative practice, a preventative approach and user involvement.

Case Study 1: Imani Project, NCH Action for Children

In regard to the sub-indicators outlined above, this case study was chosen from the list of possible NCH Action for Children projects as the most representative of issues for women and children from minority ethnic communities and because it includes an emphasis on:

- equality policies
- safety
- empowerment
- listening to the voices of service users.

The work of the project

Imani is situated in the centre of a multi-racial area in the south west of London. It offers individual and group support to women and children experiencing domestic violence, providing community-based services including:

- a women's support group
- a general women's drop-in
- a specific drop-in dealing with abuse
- one-to-one advocacy and support.

In all domestic violence cases dealt with by the police, the woman is given information on Imani. The advocacy work attempts to be practically strengthening to women who have experienced violence, opening options so that women can make their own decisions in a more powerful way. Imani stays in contact to provide a 'cradle' of support through an ongoing link in the long term, with the aim of empowering each woman to make positive changes (not necessarily to leave home). The groups which are offered are confidential and operate within a safe and secure venue. Specific children's services and support are provided, with children's groupwork currently planned and individual support for children and their mothers forming part of ongoing provision.

The idea of the groups and the individual support offered is to provide a place where coordinated advocacy and support is available, to prevent women from being sent from agency to agency.

Local partnership links

The project is a partnership between NCH Action for Children and Battersea Central Mission, and has also taken an active part in the local domestic violence forum, assisting in producing a crisis pack, for example, and attempting to obtain funding for a forum coordinator. The philosophy of the project is to be 'upfront' about the work which they do – to be seen by the community and by others to be doing this work.

Underlying principles

The project uses a comprehensive definition of domestic violence. NCH Action for Children provides training and assistance, which is viewed as essential to the functioning of the programme.

Overall, Imani is a community development project which engages in very practical down-to-earth empowerment. It avoids the use of jargon, but couches everything in terms of giving women more tools to make decisions and more practical power in their own lives, including through mutual support. Women who have gone through refuges or who have otherwise moved on to strong new lives are invited back (expenses paid) to give women currently using the services optimism – to be a beacon of hope. The whole project has an empowerment ethos, but in a very practical and detailed, small-scale way, focusing on one particular community.

An awareness of power, control and gender issues runs through the project but is not talked about in sociological ways. Rather Imani looks at *how* power and control play themselves out in women's lives practically. All the 'thinking' is aware of gender, but in concrete ways.

Safety

Imani makes detailed safety plans with abused women and children and safety issues are always at the forefront of their work (see Good Practice Indicator 4).

Equalities and service users' voices

The project is open to all women and makes this clear (for example, all women using the service are given a short version of the full equality policy). The name itself was chosen because it has resonance in various Asian and African languages. Also, the name is reassuring to black women who may not wish to go to the police or social services, and leads them to realise that there is a project out there for them specifically.

Imani works with women of all heritages including African, African-Caribbean, Asian, Chinese and white women, and has good links with refuges for black women in the area, some of which have outreach projects. All work done is sensitive to cultural issues in a very detailed and open way. They talk openly about the mix of women using the project and are visible in the community in this respect.

Monitoring, evaluation and cost-effectiveness

The project monitors its services to some extent, but has not been evaluated (an evaluation is planned for 2000). The feedback of women users is generally positive. Although small-scale (with only one full-time worker), Imani believes that its services may save agencies money by doing the groundwork on their behalf, offering practical empowerment and down-to-earth community support. Equalities and cultural awareness are to the fore in everything the project does. Imani demonstrates a positive role for NCH Action for Children, and could not operate without their helpful back-up.

Case Study 2: Wyrley Birch Centre for Parents and Children

This case study demonstrates many areas of good practice although it is particularly relevant to the sub-indicators of:

- children's needs and voices
- mainstreaming services.

The work of the project

The Wyrley Birch Centre is run by The Children's Society in Birmingham. Established initially as a general family centre, Wyrley Birch has developed its work in relation to domestic violence to the point where it has become widely respected as a centre of expertise in working with women and children who have lived with domestic violence, and in training staff of other agencies to think about the effects of domestic violence on children. Its work has been evaluated positively within a qualitative, action research framework. This form of evaluation allows for ongoing feedback and continued development of the service.

The project offers a range of services for parents

or carers including pre-school provision and after-school and holiday activities. Wyrley Birch holds a service level agreement with Birmingham City Council to carry out individual casework with families where domestic violence has been identified as an issue.

Children's voices and mainstreaming

The staff also run children's groups at local refuges, giving children an important and unique opportunity to talk about their experiences, thoughts and feelings. Wyrley Birch is involved with Birmingham Women's Aid and the West Midlands Probation Service in providing groups to support women and children when their abusers are attending a perpetrators' programme. This has recently extended to providing a direct input into the perpetrators' group on parenting issues, confronting men with the impact of their abusive behaviour on their children.

This commitment to carrying the voice of the child into mainstream practice has been further pursued through the use of drama. A training presentation developed by Wyrley Birch staff focuses on the story of 'Jade', an eight-year-old girl who is portrayed as having come to a refuge with her mother. The role play is used to illustrate all the issues experienced by a child living with, and then escaping, domestic violence, and has formed the basis of regular contributions to ACPC multi-agency training over a three-year period. The child's perspective has also been conveyed through practice, including in the courts, and through the centre's participation in two local domestic violence forums.

At the same time, staff have been instrumental in seeking to mainstream domestic violence awareness throughout their own agency – The Children's Society – by ensuring that specialist training is made available on domestic violence and child protection.

Case Study 3: Domestic Violence Outreach Scheme, Northern Ireland

This project is featured because of its direct work with both women and children, including that on safety issues. It is located in light, modern premises behind an anonymous doorway and is handy for transport both to local towns and into a rural hinterland. One room is very child-centred, the other has work displayed on the walls from women's discussions of what domestic violence means to them.

Direct work with children is divided into 'safety work' – offered while the danger from the perpetrator is still real – and 'recovery work' – which is undertaken when the children have moved into a safer phase of their lives but when they still have many issues to deal with.

Safety work

Safety work focuses on thorough safety planning, as illustrated by the example quoted under Good Practice Indicator 4. One nine-year-old girl who was interviewed said it had made a lot of difference to her to do the work because she had found it useful to talk to the workers: "Otherwise", she said, "you think about it at school and your work gets messy". Since receiving help from the project, her school work had improved and she had been able to talk to family members about other confusing things in her life.

Recovery work

Recovery work takes the form of groupwork based on a model developed in North America. Children learn to recognise, name and accept their own feelings, however intense and mixed up these may be, through the use of age-appropriate games, drawings and so on. They make sense of what has happened in their lives and come to understand that it is not their fault. Once again, talking to the workers about what has been a family secret can be very reassuring. In this project, mothers attend their own group in parallel with the one for children. It is particularly helpful for them to hear which key message the children are working on each week so that they can carry on the good work at home, for example, "It's okay to talk and let out your feelings", and, "Sometimes I'm mad at my mummy for not finding a way to make things better ... this is okay".

Working with women and children

A crucial part of the project's overall approach is to understand that work with children can get nowhere unless there are also services for women, to help them rebuild a safe and fulfilling life both for themselves and their children. The project runs a 16-week women's group, aimed at educating and empowering women to deal more effectively with domestic violence in their lives, and also offers individual counselling. There is a follow-on support group for women who frequently use it to help them move on and take courses, become volunteers in the project, or find other ways to rebuild their lives on their own terms. Women's safety is monitored with them every time they attend, and they have their own detailed safety plans in place. Women from across the sectarian divide discuss issues together such as child contact, their experiences of court, benefits entitlements, solicitors, the continuing dangers from perpetrators and the needs of their children. The nine women the research team member had the opportunity to meet were clearly determined to do the best for their children and recognised that the project saw helping mothers as crucial. Accolades for the project included:

> "The main thing was just being believed when I came here."

> "It really grounded me, getting down to basics about locks, the police, having a 'phone by the bed with a light on it."

> "The first group that gave me hope."

> "I feel comfortable to talk about anything or I don't have to talk."

Service user involvement

The project's steering group has women service users forming at least half of its membership. They feel their ideas are genuinely listened and responded to, and that changes have come about as a result. For example, in a meeting with a newly referred or self-referred woman child protection policies are no longer the very first thing mentioned, before she has had a chance to decide whether or not she trusts the workers. Rather, child protection concerns form an integral part of the work and having clear expectations and boundaries ensures that the project can support women with child protection issues by making safety for both children and women a key factor in intervention.

Case Study 4: NSPCC Family Support Project in Hayle

This case study was selected because it provides an example of joint work between the NSPCC and Women's Aid with children and their mothers in a rural setting. The project fulfils the criteria of:

- empowering users' voices
- emphasising the needs of children
- building safety
- inter-agency working.

Local partnership

The NSPCC Family Support Project in Hayle offers services to children, parents and carers in the Penwith area of Cornwall. Despite having only two full-time members of staff supplemented by several trainee children's workers, the project works in a variety of ways in partnership with the community to improve safety and quality of life for local children. It does this through promoting positive parenting, increasing awareness of child safety and giving children a voice within the community.

Family support

The general approach of the service is that of 'family support', rather than the child protection investigation or abuse recovery and treatment work carried out by many other NSPCC services (see Hester and Pearson, 1998). The emphasis is therefore on helping parents to parent effectively and on providing children with the 'normal' play activities and experiences that they may have missed out on, for whatever reason, including living in circumstances of domestic violence. Work with mothers and children on domestic violence in most of the groups thus tends to be indirect, with the various groups providing a safe place which facilitates disclosure of domestic and other abuse.

Both the Women's Aid refuge and NSPCC feel that the importance of this approach is that the NSPCC are working in the 'in-between-field', between the child protection activities of social services and the teaching of skills – and this allows child abuse, domestic violence and family issues to be considered together.

The NSPCC and Women's Aid children's group

The children's group run jointly with the local Women's Aid refuge for children living in the refuge was set up four years ago. The NSPCC and refuge were originally housed in the same premises and this led to close inter-agency links which continued when the refuge moved to their own premises. The refuge has always emphasised the importance of inter-agency links, and, consequently, its staff are seen locally as the experts on domestic violence and part of the children and families 'team'. The NSPCC project is also committed to inter-agency working.

Focused play activity

The joint children's group in the refuge is run once a week with a member of staff from the NSPCC and the childcare workers from the refuge. The joint group was initially set up with the idea of working with mothers, but quickly developed into a specific children's group as there was a pressing need for the development of focused play activity with children. The NSPCC worker brings particular skills concerning children's development and play behaviour. As is the situation for many children living with domestic violence, the children in the refuge have often taken on responsibilities for protection of their mothers and/or siblings and have developed a variety of strategies for coping. They may be mature for their years and may have missed out on fun and play. At the same time, there is often a wide age range of children in the group and children may only stay in the refuge for a short while. The group thus emphasises activities that build the ability to play and have fun in the longer term.

Indirect work with children concerning their experiences of domestic violence and abuse is also carried out using, for instance, a 'brick wall' where children can write whatever concerns them, and which can then be looked at in the group, leading to support and understanding from the other children as well as from staff. Children who need further therapeutic work are referred outside the project.

Case Study 5: Hereford Women's Aid, Hereford

Hereford Women's Aid was selected as an example of a women's refuge and outreach service, fulfilling various of the case study criteria/practice sub-indicators including:

- mainstreaming
- users' voices
- equalities
- children's services
- safety
- cost-effectiveness
- monitoring.

The project provides refuge and outreach services from a purpose-designed building, as well as a comprehensive children's project and aftercare. A separate advice centre as a 'public face' in the city is planned. Hereford Women's Aid is affiliated to WAFE; it has been in existence for many years and has a strong local profile. The group considers the following issues to be key to good domestic violence practice:

- clear, considered policies;
- clear and straightforward communication;
- clear rules on safety and confidentiality;
- firm and consistent application of policies and guidelines both within Hereford Women's Aid and the multi-agency context.

Mainstreaming and local partnerships

Considerable effort has been put into getting the issue of domestic violence fully accepted as an integral part of policy development in the statutory sector locally. For example, Hereford Women's Aid was asked to lead a task group to produce a domestic violence protocol in relation to the Children's Services Plan. This has led to the adoption of statutory practice guidelines, in conjunction with the ACPC. The group has wide-ranging relationships with other local agencies and is seen as a key stakeholder in local activity on domestic violence.

Equalities

The services provided are open to all sections of the local community: there is good disabled access and provision, and specific projects for disabled women have been conducted. A separate space is available for women without children. The county is mainly white but outreach is conducted to small, local Chinese and Asian populations.

Voices of service users

The group is run with a collective structure, including a small management committee. The key worker system and weekly house meetings allow the views of women resident in the refuge to be expressed and fed into the staff meeting. In addition, the regular meetings of the collective are open to all residents or their representatives, and the agenda for these meetings is discussed at house meetings. Exit questionnaires are completed by all women leaving. Additionally, some members of staff and management are survivors of domestic violence themselves and can thus contribute a relevant perspective.

The collective is a visible attempt to share power and control, and to empower women who have experienced domestic violence and their children. However, it is recognised that differences in status, money and power between workers and women service users are a structural factor and that the most important counter to this must be a constant process of awareness and listening. There is an identified need for the local domestic violence forum to be more responsive to women and children's voices, and attempts are being made to address this need, possibly through establishing focus groups.

Safety

The refuge was purpose built with safety as a key feature (see Good Practice Indicator 4).

Children's services

A well-equipped purpose-designed playroom is part of the new building and an extensive children's programme is offered by the children's workers with daily play sessions. Play is seen as crucial in enabling children to overcome experiences of abuse. There are outings and holidays, a separate lounge exists for the teenagers with a PlayStation, and counselling support is offered. The approach of the children's workers is to work with children and mothers to build up trusting relationships with both, with the aim of respecting and empowering mothers in their childcare, and enabling children to feel that their views are heard and represented.

Systematic monitoring, evaluation and cost effectiveness

Statistical data is systematically collected and recorded, and selected statistics are available to the public. The refuge has a service agreement with social services and the housing authority under which its services are evaluated by a multi-agency steering group. No formal outside evaluation has been conducted to date, but feedback from service users is always considered.

As with most Women's Aid groups, the refuge existed for many years before domestic violence moved towards the mainstream. From a small pressure group many years ago, Hereford Women's Aid has become accepted by statutory bodies and by the community as the major domestic violence resource in the area. This success has brought its own problems, such as pressures on time, space, finance and the small number of dedicated workers. Funding shortage is an enduring issue, but the group has achieved much over a long period of committed service provision and activism on domestic violence in the Hereford area.

Case Studies 6 and 7: Fife and the London Borough of Newham

These case studies were selected as examples of statutory authorities where domestic violence work was being mainstreamed and where substantial service development had taken place. It was considered more appropriate to describe these developments in the body of the report, as the work does not refer to a specific, ring-fenced project, but rather facets of innovative, domestic violence work within a large statutory organisation. Reference to Fife is made throughout this report. Reference to Newham is made in Chapter 2 under the **Social services departments** section (pp 13-18).

49

5

Conclusion and recommendations

Domestic violence mapping

Variation in service provision

The clearest finding from the mapping questionnaires is, not surprisingly, that the development of provision at local level is extremely varied. Some areas showed excellent levels of provision and the development of policies and training to guide practice.

An interesting mix of strategies at local and national levels appears to have been used to galvanise policy and practice developments. Through this process, innovative practice at local level has often acted as a catalyst for the development of national policy within organisations, which in turn seeks to 'trickle down' by developing training, writing specific policies, distributing resources or shifting priorities to take domestic violence into account. This process also works across organisations where the lead from one organisation (or from individual workers) can create the impetus for change in another. Conversely, the lack of priority given to domestic violence by key organisations in a local area can also act as a deterrent to the development of service provision and more effective intervention strategies.

The extreme level of variation in service provision and policy development raises serious questions about inequality and resources – 20% of questionnaires to social services departments said that there was no provision for work with children, women or men in situations of domestic violence in their area. Specific service provision for children living in situations of domestic violence features in only 20% of Children's Services Plans. Similar points could be made about levels of training and policy development. More than 30% of local authorities and 50% of children's charities projects have not provided even the most basic half- or one-day awareness training on domestic violence to staff. A total of 45% of social services departments have not developed domestic violence policy guidelines and 84% of children's charities' projects also lack policies to guide practice in this area. These figures on policy are all the more surprising when, at national level, all the children's charities have developed excellent policy and practice guidelines, and the DoH has been proactive in highlighting the issue in a range of guidance to social services departments.

On a more optimistic note, the consistency and extent of provision across Northern Ireland is higher than in England and Wales and is indicative of the potential to progress work in this area. Scotland has recently allocated direct state funding of £8 million to further work in this area. It should also be recognised that although there is very significant work to be done to raise the quantity and the quality of service provision with regard to domestic violence, a similar survey 10 years earlier would have shown minimal provision and development anywhere except through the specialist services provided by organisations such as Women's Aid.

Currently, Women's Aid and other women's refuges and support, advocacy and outreach services form a national network across the UK and demonstrate good practice overall, although hampered by poor, or inadequate resources.

Recommendation

These findings raise questions about whether national minimum standards for domestic violence provision need to be addressed to bring greater equity into the area. The Women's Unit of the Cabinet Office and Home Office document, *Living without fear* (1999), the current Home Office Crime Reduction Programme on domestic violence, and the work of the inter-departmental governmental group which meets to monitor progress on domestic violence provision in England and Wales have underpinned their work by drawing on examples of good practice. These may not be sufficient to address the serious problems of inequity and inadequate resourcing, without an underpinning strategy which addresses minimum standards.

A framework for good practice for working with families where there is domestic violence

A framework of eight good practice indicators, each with a series of sub-indicators, was developed on the basis of the following data: 915 questionnaires which formed the main part of the mapping project; the seven case studies; consultancy with relevant organisations; and the consultations between the research team and the advisory group. The framework is applicable at both strategic and operational levels. Clearly some indicators will apply more fully at the strategic level to set the context for good practice, while others will be more easily embedded at an operational or practice level in relation to work with children, women and men in situations of domestic violence.

*Good Practice Indicator 1: Definitions –
setting the parameters*

The development of a **definition of domestic violence** to set the parameters for policy and practice development in the organisation and multi-agency context. Definitions need to:

* acknowledge diversity and the gendered nature of domestic violence, and include different types of abuse;
* provide recognition of domestic violence as an abuse of power and control of one person by another.

Good Practice Indicator 2: Monitoring and screening – knowing the extent of the problem

Monitoring and screening allow domestic violence to be recorded, studied and assessed, and assist abused women and children in 'naming' the issue. They can be achieved through:

* **systematic screening using a protocol of questions** which emphasise behaviours rather than initially asking directly about domestic violence;
* **mechanisms for recording** domestic violence;
* **guidance and supervision** for frontline practitioners;
* **training** associated with the introduction of screening and monitoring;
* **feedback mechanisms** for using the monitoring data.

Good Practice Indicator 3: Policies and guidelines – guiding the work to be done

Domestic violence policies and guidelines provide a consistent framework for the work to be undertaken. Policies need to:

* emphasise **safety** and clarify the issues of **confidentiality**;
* **involve survivors of domestic violence** and their representatives in refuge and advocacy services;
* give attention to **diversity and equalities** issues;
* develop the particular organisational policies **in conjunction with a wider multi-agency strategy**;
* develop **a broad range of policies and guidelines** for work with children and families, vulnerable adults and community care recipients, perpetrators, practice guidelines for frontline workers, safety policies for workers and policies specific for each department and organisation;
* **build on policies** which have already been well developed in other areas;
* **embed policies within the organisation** through training, guidance, appropriate procedural developments and service provision;
* include **detailed guidelines**, which explicate the issues for practice.

Good Practice Indicator 4: Safety measures and safety-oriented practice

Safety planning needs to include:

- **safety planning** with individuals who may face violence and abuse;
- **ensuring the safety of women and children through a range of measures** at the organisational level aimed at stopping violence or minimising risk;
- **supporting and ensuring the safety of mothers** as a means of protecting and enhancing the welfare of children;
- organisational measures to **ensure worker's safety**.

Good Practice Indicator 5: Training – raising awareness, exploring values, developing skills

Domestic violence training and awareness-raising can be used to develop skills and values and to embed policy. Training needs to include:

- a strategy for **training large numbers of employees** in an organisation;
- **awareness raising** combined with **a range of specialist courses**;
- **a rolling programme** of domestic violence training;
- the **integration of the training strategy** into the broader strategic planning for domestic violence intervention;
- secure **financial resources** for domestic violence training;
- attention to **training quality**.

Good Practice Indicator 6: Evaluation – ensuring effective provision

The framework of indicators listed above provide parameters for evaluation, with different considerations applying to evaluating work with survivors on the one hand, and work with perpetrators on the other. Sub-indicators of good practice in respect of evaluation in the field of domestic violence have been identified as the following:

- **independent evaluation** conducted by evaluators with a knowledge of domestic violence issues, in conjunction with practitioners themselves;
- **building in the voice of survivors** for both women and/or children;

- **follow-up** to ensure that women and children remain safe;
- **feedback loop** to examine 'what works' and also to identify areas of practice which need to change.

Good Practice Indicator 7: Multi-agency coordination – working together.

Multi-agency strategies can be used to coordinate the development of policy and practice across organisations within an area. Such strategies should include:

- attention to **consistency of services and policies** across and within agencies;
- attention to issues of **confidentiality and agreement** in relation to women and children service users;
- full and active **involvement of women's refuge, outreach and support services**;
- attention to **equality issues and effective mechanisms for active consultation** with service users;
- **clarity** of lines of accountability, responsibility and actions undertaken;
- **monitoring** of effectiveness and evaluation of inter-agency coordination;
- measurable improvements in **resourcing** (including domestic violence coordinators).

Good Practice Indicator 8: Guidelines for practical working with women and children

All practice interventions need to include a practical focus on the needs of women and children experiencing domestic violence. While all the above dimensions of good practice will apply, specific sub-indicators for practice work will include the underpinning of work by the assumption that **supporting women is often an effective means of supporting and protecting children**, while acknowledging that **children and women's needs and experiences are different and require separate, but linked, provision**. The sub-indicators include:

- **attention to the voices and expressed needs of the women using the service** (and their active involvement where possible) so that provision is sensitively attuned to their needs;
- **attention to children's needs and views** in terms of preventative work on abuse with

children, as well as child protection issues;

- **the empowerment of abused women and children** so that they are enabled to build effective responses to abuse and positive future lives;
- **attempts to mainstream the service** so that concrete and empowering work with abused women and children spreads across all sectors;
- **monitoring and evaluation** to ensure effective provision.

General principles underlying all provision and service development with abused women and children include:

- the **first and main priority to be improvements in safety**;
- the adoption of **a believing, sensitive approach**;
- the **provision and delivery of effective services**;
- the **development of specific and diverse services** in relation to **minority ethnic and other communities**.

While this framework is a useful beginning, it is not exhaustive – particularly as good practice in the area of domestic violence involves housing, policing, legal issues, health and education. It is difficult to divorce the 'family work' from these wider contexts and organisations. The good practice guidelines for perpetrator programmes have been developed by RESPECT.

Recommendation

The framework of indicators of good practice for working with children, women and men where there is domestic violence should be adopted as a national framework by the government, and by the statutory, charitable and independent sectors to guide domestic violence practice and policy development.

Future directions

The project has pointed to a number of areas in which future research could be used as a means of progressing policy development and practice in the area of work with families where there is domestic violence.

- Given the variation in provision across the sector, developing action research projects and other studies to evaluate and understand in more detail the opportunities and barriers to the development of particular services and strategies would be opportune. For example:
  - developing the use of definitions, and of monitoring and screening for domestic violence across sectors;
  - tracking the implementation and effects of a domestic violence training strategy within an organisation or inter-agency forum;
  - tracking the process and effects of the development and implementation of domestic violence protocols and procedures (for example, in relation to child abuse);
  - tracking and evaluating the use of comprehensive domestic violence strategies across a locality;
  - tracking the use of detailed safety planning with abused women and children.
- This research could be built on to address the issue of minimum standards of domestic violence policy implementation and service provision for each local authority area.
- A number of local authorities have allocated funds for a designated domestic violence worker. Evaluating the effectiveness of this development would be timely.
- A wide range of policies in relation to confidentiality and referral are developing within different multi-agency contexts. A project to audit and evaluate best practice in this area using several contrasting multi-agency sites would point directions for future practice.
- Services for women and children are currently diversifying beyond refuge provision to meet the needs of wider groups of women and children. Different models for outreach are emerging. The effectiveness of these strategies needs to be evaluated from the perspective of service users.

- The co-occurrence of domestic violence and child abuse in many cases is gaining increased recognition across the sector. Studies which research this dimension in more detail are still required in the UK.
- The consistent evaluation of perpetrator programmes is needed along a range of dimensions, including funding for comprehensive longitudinal studies.
- There are areas not covered in this research which impact on family support services in the area of domestic violence. In particular, post-separation violence and the role of supported and supervised contact centres have not been explored in this project; however, this is an area that requires research attention.

The impressive level of cooperation at all levels within this project – the workers who filled in the 915 questionnaires, the children's charities and Women's Aid, the various research centres involved, the different countries across the UK, the advisory group and the collaborative, cross-institutional team of researchers – provide cause for optimism that work will continue to progress and develop in working with children, women and men where there is domestic violence. This project points to areas of great strength, undreamt of 15 years ago, as well as significant gaps in the development of this work.

References

Abrahams, C. (1994) *The hidden victims – Children and domestic violence*, London: NCH Action for Children.

Atkinson, C. (1996) 'Partnership working – supporting those who work with the children of domestic violence', Paper given to the Behind Closed Doors Seminar, 'The effects of domestic violence on children and vulnerable young people', Thames Valley.

Ball, M. (1995) *Domestic violence and social care: A report on two conferences held by the Social Services Inspectorate*, London: DoH.

Barnardo's (1997) Domestic Violence Policy and Strategy Document, London: Barnado's.

Barnardo's, NSPCC and University of Bristol (1998) *Making an impact: Children and domestic violence, training pack*, London: Barnardo's in association with DoH.

Bath and North East Somerset Housing and Social Services Department (1999) *Child care quality manual*, Bath: Bath and North East Somerset Council.

Bedfordshire County Council (1999) *Good practice in working with families where there is domestic violence*, Bedford: Bedfordshire Social and Community Care.

Brasse, V. (2000) *Resource manual for health services*, London: DoH.

Burton, S., Regan, L. and Kelly, L. (1998) *Supporting women and challenging men: Lessons from the Domestic Violence Intervention Project*, Bristol/York: The Policy Press/Joseph Rowntree Foundation.

Casey, M. (1989) *Domestic violence against women: The women's perspective*, Dublin: Social Psychology Research Unit, University College Dublin.

Cheshire County Council (1998) *Domestic violence policy and guidelines*, Cheshire: Cheshire County Council.

City of Bradford (undated) *Women experiencing violence from known men: Policy and practice guidelines*, Bradford: Bradford Social Service.

Coventry City Council (1999) *Action on domestic violence in Coventry*, Coventry: Coventry City Council.

Debbonaire, T. (1994) 'Work with children in Women's Aid refuges and after', in A. Mullender and R. Morley (eds) *Children living with domestic violence*, London: Whiting and Birch.

DoH (Department of Health) (1995) *Child protection: Messages from research*, London: HMSO.

DoH (1997) *Local Authority Circular: Family Law Act 1996, Part IV Family homes and domestic violence*, London: DoH.

DoH (1999a) *Working together to safeguard children*, Consultative draft, London: DoH.

DoH (1999b) *The Family Law Act 1996 Domestic Violence Survey Report on Local Authority Implementation of Part IV*, London: DoH.

Dobash, R. and Dobash, R.E. (1992) *Women, violence and social change*, London: Routledge.

Dobash, R., Dobash, R.E., Cavanagh, K. and Lewis, R. (1996) *Research evaluation of programmes for violent men*, Edinburgh: HMSO.

Doncaster Metropolitan Borough Council (1997) *Doncaster Domestic Violence Working Party Manual*, Doncaster: Metropolitan Borough Council.

DSS (Department of Social Security) (1998) *Supporting people: A new policy and framework for support services*, London: Crown Publications.

Fife Multi-agency Domestic Violence Forum (1996) *Domestic violence in Fife: A report of the Equal Opportunities Working Group in Fife*, Fife: Fife Council.

Fife Multi-agency Domestic Violence Forum (1999) *Working together to challenge domestic violence*, Fife: Fife Council.

Gittins, D. (1985) *The family in question: Changing households and familiar ideologies*, Basingstoke: Macmillan.

Gloucestershire Social Services (1999) *Department policy on domestic violence*, Gloucester: Gloucestershire Social Services.

Gondolf, E. (1997) 'Batterer programs: what we know and need to know', *Journal of Interpersonal Violence*, vol 12, no 1, pp 83-98.

Gondolf, E. (1998a) 'The impact of mandatory court review on batterer program compliance: and evaluation of the Pittsburgh Municipal Courts and Domestic Abuse Counselling Centre. Executive summary, at www.iup.edu/maati/publications

Gondolf, E. (1998b) 'Multi-site evaluation of batterer intervention systems: reliability and validity of outcome measures for batterer intervention evaluation', at www.iup.edu/maati/publications

Hague, G. and Malos, E. (1996) *Tackling domestic violence: A guide to multi-agency initiatives on domestic violence*, Bristol/York: The Policy Press/Joseph Rowntree Foundation.

Hague, G. and Malos, E. (1998) *Domestic violence: Action for change*. 2nd edn, Cheltenham: New Clarion Press.

Hague, G., Kelly, L., Malos, E. and Mullender, A. with Debbonaire, T. (1996a) *Children, domestic violence and refuges: A study of needs and responses*, Bristol: WAFE.

Hague, G., Malos, E. and Dear, W. (1996b) *Multi-agency work and domestic violence*, Bristol/York: The Policy Press/Joseph Rowntree Foundation.

Hague, G., Mullender, A., Aris, R. and Dear, W. (forthcoming) *Abused women's perspectives: Responsiveness and accountability of domestic violence and inter-agency initiatives*, Bristol: School for Policy Studies, University of Bristol.

Harwin, N., Hague, G. and Malos, E. (eds) (1999) *The multi-agency approach to domestic violence: New opportunities, old challenges*, London: Whiting and Birch.

Henderson, S. (1997) *Service provision to women experiencing domestic violence in Scotland*, Edinburgh: The Scottish Office.

Hester, M. and Pearson, C. (1998) *From periphery to centre: Domestic violence in work with abused children*, Bristol/York: The Policy Press/Joseph Rowntree Foundation.

Hester, M and Radford, L. (1996) *Domestic violence and child contact arrangements in England and Denmark*, Bristol/York: The Policy Press/Joseph Rowntree Foundation.

Hester, M., Pearson, C. and Harwin, N. (1998) *Making an impact: Children and domestic violence – a reader*, London: Barnardo's in association with DoH, 2000 edition published by Jessica Kingsley.

Hester, M., Pearson, C. and Radford, L. (1997) *Domestic violence: A national survey of court welfare and voluntary sector mediation practice*, Bristol/York: The Policy Press/Joseph Rowntree Foundation.

Home Office (1999) *Policing domestic violence: Effective organisational structures*, London: Home Office.

Home Office (2000a) *Circular 19/2000, Domestic Violence*, London: Home Office.

Home Office (2000b) *Multi-agency guidance for addressing domestic violence*, London: Home Office.

Home Office and Welsh Office (1995) *Inter-agency Circular: Inter-agency co-ordination to tackle domestic violence*, London: Home Office.

House of Commons Home Affairs Committee (1993) *Report of Inquiry into Domestic Violence*, London: HMSO.

Humphreys, C. (2000) *Social work, domestic violence and child protection: Challenging practice*, Bristol: The Policy Press.

Kelly, L. (1999) *Domestic violence matters: An evaluation of a development project*, Home Office Study 188, London: The Stationery Office.

Leeds City Council Department of Social Services (undated) *Good practice guidelines, policy and guidance notes: Women experiencing violence from known men*, Leeds: Leeds City Council.

London Borough of Croydon (1999) *One Stop Shop*, London: London Borough of Croydon.

London Borough of Hackney (1993) *The links between domestic violence and child abuse: Developing services*, London: Hackney Council Press and Publicity Team.

London Borough of Hammersmith and Fulham (1995) *Making the difference*, London: London Borough of Hammersmith and Fulham.

London Borough of Hammersmith and Fulham (1998) *Responding with respect*, London: London Borough of Hammersmith and Fulham.

London Borough of Islington (1995, revised edn) *Working with those who have experienced domestic violence: A good practice guide*, London: London Borough of Islington Women's Equality Unit.

London Borough of Newham (1994-97) *Community Care Plan*, London: London Borough of Newham.

McGee, C. (2000) *Childhood experiences of domestic violence*, London: Jessica Kingsley.

McWilliams, M. and McKiernan, J. (1993) *Bringing it out in the open: Domestic violence in Northern Ireland*, Belfast: HMSO.

Morran, D. and Wilson, M. (1997) *Men who are violent to women: A groupwork practice manual*, Lyme Regis: Russell House Publishing.

Mullender, A. (1996) *Rethinking domestic violence: The social work and probation response*, London: Routledge.

Mullender, A. (1999) 'Social service responses to domestic violence: the inter-agency challenge,' in N. Harwin, G. Hague and E. Malos (eds) *Domestic violence and multi-agency working: New opportunities, old challenges?*, London: Whiting and Birch.

Mullender, A. and Burton, S. (2000) 'What works with perpetrators', in J. Taylor-Browne (ed) *Reducing domestic violence: What works?*, London: Home Office Research and Statistics Directorate.

Mullender, A. and Humphreys, C. with Saunders, H. (1998) *Domestic violence and child abuse: Policy and practice issues for local authorities and other agencies*, Briefing paper from the task group on domestic violence and child abuse, London: Local Government Association.

Mullender, A. and Morley, R. (eds) (1994) *Children living with domestic violence: Putting men's abuse of women on the child care agenda*, London: Whiting and Birch.

National Inter-agency Working Party Report (1992) *Domestic violence*, London: Victim Support.

NFM (National Family Mediation) (1998) *National Family Mediation policy on domestic violence*, London: NFM.

NCAVAC (National Campaign Against Violence and Crime Unit) (1998) *Ending domestic violence?: Programs for perpetrators, summary volume*, Canberra, Australia: NCAVAC Unit, Attorney-General's Department.

NCH Action for Children (1997) *Making a difference: Working with women and children experiencing domestic violence*, London: NCH Action for Children.

NIWA (Northern Ireland Women's Aid) (1998a) *No fear, heading for healthy relationships: An activity pack for working with young people*, Belfast: NIWA.

NIWA (1998b)*Violence on the edge: Providing effective support for minority ethnic women at risk of domestic violence in Northern Ireland*, Belfast: NIWA.

Parkinson, P. and Humphreys, C. (1998) 'Children who witness domestic violence: the implications for child protection', *Child and Family Law Quarterly*, vol 10, no 2, pp 147-59.

Patton, M.Q. (1990) *Qualitative evaluation and research methods*, Thousand Oaks, CA: Sage Publications.

Pence, E. and Paymar, M. (1996, revised edn) *Education groups for men who batter: The Duluth model*, New York, NY: Springer.

Pryke, J. and Thomas, T. (1998) *Domestic violence and social work*, Aldershot: Ashgate Publishing.

RESPECT (2000) 'Statement of principles and minimum standards of practice', held at DVIP, PO Box 2838, London W6 9ZE.

Scottish Home and Health Department (1990) 'Investigation of complaints of domestic assault', Circular 3/1990, Edinburgh: Scottish Home and Health Department.

Scottish Office (1998) *Guidance on preparing and implementing a multi-agency strategy to tackle violence against women*, COSLA Report, Edinburgh: Scottish Office.

Scottish Women's Aid (1999) *Young people speak out about domestic violence*, Volumes 1 and 2, Edinburgh: Scottish Women's Aid.

Scottish Women's Aid (2000) *National overview of the first Scottish Children's Services Plans in relation to children and young people experiencing domestic abuse*, Edinburgh: Scottish Women's Aid.

Scourfield, J. and Dobash, R.P. (1999) 'Programmes for violent men: recent developments in the UK', *The Howard Journal of Criminal Justice*, vol 38, no 2, pp 128-43.

Shaw, I. (1996) *Evaluating in practice*, Aldershot, Ashgate Publishing.

Stanko, E.A., Crisp, D., Hale, C. and Lucraft, H. (1998) *Counting the costs: Estimating the impact of domestic violence in the London Borough of Hackney*, London: Crime Concern.

Taylor-Browne, J. (ed) (2000) *Reducing domestic violence: What works?*, London: Home Office Research and Statistics Directorate.

Tolman, R.M. and Edleson, J.L. (1995) 'Intervention for men who batter: a review of research', in S.R. Stith, and M.A. Straus (eds) *Understanding partner violence: Prevalence, causes, consequences and solutions*, Minneapolis, MN: National Council on Family Relations.

Tunstill, J. (1997) 'Implementing the family support clauses of the 1989 Children Act: legislation, professional and organisational obstacles', in N. Parton (ed) *Child protection and family support*, London: Routledge.

United Nations (1989) *Convention on the Rights of the Child: Adopted by the General Assembly of the United Nations, 1989*, London: HMSO.

Warwickshire Social Services Department (1999) *Domestic violence guidance for social work staff*, Warwick: Warwickshire Social Services Department.

WAFE (Women's Aid Federation of England) (1997) *Building blocks: A Women's Aid guide to running refuge and support services*, Bristol: WAFE Publications.

WAFE (1999a) *Families without fear*, Bristol: WAFE Publications.

WAFE (1999b) *Strengthening diversity: Good practice in delivering domestic violence to black women and children*, Bristol: WAFE Publications.

Women's Unit of the Cabinet Office and Home Office (1999) *Living without fear: An integrated approach to tackling violence against women*, London: Women's Unit and Cabinet Office.

Zero Tolerance Charitable Trust (1998*) Young people's attitudes towards violence, sex and relationships*, Edinburgh: Zero Tolerance Charitable Trust.

Appendix: Methodology

This study was made possible by the unique collaboration of the research team with other organisations involved in researching and/or providing services to families where there is domestic violence. The research partnerships with WAFE, NSPCC, Barnardo's, NCH Action for Children and The Children's Society meant that the mapping survey of family support service provision could build on each organisation's own expertise and knowledge of their services. The collaboration with the Child and Women Abuse Studies Unit, North London University, meant that the research team could draw on their evaluative work on the service provision of projects which challenge perpetrators of abuse. In addition, the research team worked closely with the DETR and with the DoH wherever possible, to make maximum use of existing and current surveys of service provision in this area.

The research was divided into two main stages. First, mapping surveys were conducted of services provided throughout the UK. This was followed by seven in-depth case studies. For both stages, quantitative and qualitative data collected was supplemented by telephone and personal interviews and consultations with various projects and departments, both locally and nationally, by documentary analysis of policies and practices, and by the use of secondary sources.

Stage 1: The mapping surveys

The research team, in collaboration with the partnership organisations, developed different questionnaires to be sent to each type of project. Each questionnaire was piloted first, and adapted to incorporate any suggestions made. In total there were five questionnaires:

- statutory sector
- Women's Aid organisations
- children's charities
- probation services perpetrators' groups
- voluntary sector perpetrators' groups.

Some adaptations were also made to make the questionnaires relevant to the different countries involved, especially in relation to differing legislation. The questionnaire surveys in the mapping study were supplemented by analysis of documentation and by interviews and consultation with key national experts in the area.

The social services questionnaire was sent out by post to the directors of all social services departments in England and Wales and health and social services trusts in Northern Ireland. Responsibility for the questionnaire was then delegated to the most appropriate person within the department (or local authority). Following negotiations with the Scottish Office, it was agreed that, as a significant amount of work had already been undertaken in Scotland, and another major research project was ongoing there, the project team would work from secondary sources. It was felt that if the team went ahead with the mapping survey in Scotland, this could jeopardise the return rates for both projects, and could undermine the ongoing research currently being carried out by the Joint Partnership Group in Scotland.

The WAFE questionnaire was developed in conjunction with the DETR, and the data collected for England was utilised by both of these organisations and by the research team. WAFE sent out the questionnaire in England, and collected the data through individual telephone interviews with each project. They also undertook distribution of the questionnaire in Wales, Scotland and Northern Ireland; the data was collected by the research team through telephone interviews with every group.

The children's charities sent out the questionnaire to all their projects, and the responses were returned to the research team for analysis. CWASU sent out questionnaires to perpetrators' groups run by both the probation services and the voluntary sector. A researcher also attended a meeting of the National Practitioners' Network to raise awareness of the survey and distribute additional copies.

Apart from Women's Aid, the posted questionnaires were followed up, first by letter and then by telephone if necessary, to maximise the returns. Overall, the following response rates were achieved.

Statutory sector (England, Wales and Northern Ireland)	62%	(n = 114)
Women's Aid and other refuges	98%	(n = 326)
Children's charities	59.5%	(n = 449)
Perpetrator groups	73.1%	(n = 26)

The data from the questionnaires was input and analysed using SPSS computer software, with the exception of the data from the Women's Aid Federations. The latter data was inputted by Women's Aid and was analysed using ACCESS software, with specialised assistance from the University of Bristol Computing Service.

Many of the organisations and projects responding to the questionnaire reported that the questionnaires had, in themselves, acted as a useful basis for discussion concerning practice with families where there is domestic violence.

Stage 2: The case study research

Seven examples of innovative practice were identified from the mapping study data and through refining the evaluative criteria to apply to local projects. The selection process took the following issues into account:

- innovative practice
- meeting many of the good practice criteria
- the need for rural and urban locations

- at least one study to be drawn from each of the children's charities, Women's Aid, and the statutory sector
- reflecting a range of different types of provision
- reflecting different user groups, such as work with children, projects aimed towards minority ethnic communities, women's projects, statutory sector work, and work with perpetrators
- preventative work.

Strategies for qualitative evaluation (Patton, 1990; Shaw, 1996) were utilised including:

- selected interviews with key personnel and with service users using a semi-structured interview schedule developed in discussion with the project's advisory group;
- observation of groups or meetings where appropriate;
- collection and analysis of relevant policy documentation;
- collection of relevant data on referral, intervention and organisational evaluation of outcomes.

Initially, the selected sites were approached on the telephone. Once agreement had been obtained for their inclusion as a case study, they were asked to forward copies of relevant policies, procedures and other documentation, prior to a visit from a member of the research team. The documents were evaluated by the research team using the indicators of good practice which were developed within the conceptual framework. This included examining terms of reference, mission statements, and policy and practice guidance. Material produced for service users and for public information was also analysed by the research team.

After the completion of the documentary analysis, a member of the research team visited the site of the project to carry out interviews and, where appropriate, to observe the work being carried out. Interviews were undertaken with key personnel and, on several occasions, focus groups were held with staff members and either individual or group interviews were carried out with women (and children) who attended the projects. The latter interviews and focus groups were conducted using a list of key areas to be discussed, to ensure that sufficient and comparable data was obtained.

For the purposes of the report, only limited aspects of the case studies have been used in order to illustrate key indicators of good practice.

Development of an evaluation framework

The researchers established a conceptual framework of principles with regard to good practice through a recursive process of triangulating information from a number of different sources:

- analysis of the data from the questionnaires, as well as from the case studies later in the process;
- literature review;
- discussions with the project advisory group;
- previous work by the research team (for example, Hague et al, 1996b; Hester et al, 1998/2000; Mullender and Humphreys, 1998).

Through this process, a number of key dimensions to the work with families where there is domestic violence were identified. Indicators for good practice emerged under the following headings:

- Work underpinned by a clear definition of domestic violence
- Effective monitoring processes and screening for domestic violence
- Development of good practice guidelines and policies
- Safety measures and planning with regard to women and children
- Staff training
- Evaluation of intervention and service provision to ensure effectiveness
- Multi-agency integration and coordination
- Practical working with women and children

Attention to the issue of safety in all aspects of the work, and to the development of anti-oppressive practice which promote the particular needs of a diverse range of children, women and men were issues underpinning this framework.